Praise for

SEASONAL HERBALISM

"Lauren Morgan's *Seasonal Herbalism* is a true treasure for beginning herbalists. She shares all the basics of folk herbal practice in clear and actionable ways, making it easy to get started or expand your own herbal journey. Her passion for the plants and deep herbal wisdom come through in each chapter, providing both valuable insights and plenty of inspiration to get you making your own nourishing medicines with ease and confidence."

— *Kimberly Gallagher, herbalist, author, and co-founder of LearningHerbs*

"Spirit and nature dance together in *Seasonal Herbalism* as surely as they do in the forests and gardens where our herbal friends bloom and thrive. Lauren Morgan combines practical hands-on instruction with inspiring stories and exercises that enable the reader to connect to the plants as the living beings, elders, and healers that they truly are."

— *Dr. Deborah Frances, RN, ND, herbalist, lecturer, and author*

"A teacher filled with passion for the Earth, herbs, dreaming, and the way of wise women, Lauren Morgan has written a book filled with grounded wisdom for living more fully and more connected to all of life. If even a fraction of people on this planet embodied these teachings, our world would be transformed."

— *Christine Rose, MD, pediatrician and herbalist*

"*Seasonal Herbalism* is the call back to the natural world that is greatly needed in the current cultural climate. Lauren Morgan offers the wisdom of her education and experience with practical uses for immediate implementation while reminding us that plants and seasonal rhythms are imprinted in our DNA. *Seasonal Herbalism* is a practical guide to inspire all to step into the world we were meant for."

— *Michelle Scandalis Kyncl, herbalist and co-founder of Hierophant Meadery & Apothecary*

"In this dark night of the species soul when the forces of collapse threaten the integrity of the human soul, where can we turn for the guidance we need to navigate the rough waters? Turn to this book! In clear and honest prose, Lauren Morgan throws wide open the door to the guidance and healing powers of the plant kingdom and invites us in. I'll meet you at the threshold. Let's go!"

— *Randy Morris, PhD, professor emeritus, Antioch University Seattle*

"Lauren Morgan's *Seasonal Herbalism* is a beautiful gift that should be shared with anyone who has any interest in plant medicine or improving their relationship with plants. Her guidance is gentle, approachable, authentic, and heart-centered. Her writing helped me deepen my personal journey and connection to nature."

— *Alicia Whalen, beginner herbalist*

"*Seasonal Herbalism* awakens the dream in all who aspire to become more deeply rooted along the plant path. Lauren Morgan shows us how to walk through each season in deep connection with the local flora and how to take this wisdom into our own homes to create medicine for ourselves, our families, and our communities. If you're an aspiring herbalist, Lauren's teachings will surely inspire you to re-member and reweave your life intimately with Mother Earth and her beautiful gifts."

— *Emily Mastrianni, beginner herbalist*

"Regardless of a reader's previous exposure to herbalism, this essential seasonal guide for realignment with our Mother Earth is a template for us all to find healthy, balanced, and beautiful relationships with all of Creation."

— *Lily Ostle, herbalist and owner of De Danaan Folk Herbalism*

Seasonal Herbalism

A Beginner's Path to Medicine-Making and Dreaming with Mother Earth

Lauren Morgan

Seasonal Herbalism: A Beginner's Path to Medicine-Making and Dreaming with Mother Earth

Copyright © 2024 by Lauren Morgan

All rights reserved. No parts of this publication may be reproduced without prior permission of the copyright holder.

Cover art and illustrations copyright © 2024 by Lauren Blair Churchill, used with permission.

ISBN: 9798323505784
www.laurelcrownhealing.com

Discounts on bulk ordering are available for classes, study groups, and book groups.

The information in this book is intended for educational purposes only and should not be considered as a recommendation for any particular medical or health treatment. The author disclaims any liability in connection with the use of the information in this book. Consult a qualified health care provider before ingesting these or any herbal medicines. Never ingest any wild plant without first verifying the exact identity with an expert.

For the Good Dream of Mother Earth

Table of Contents

Introduction — 1

PART 1: The Reweaving Power of Herbalism — 7

    Chapter 1: Re-Membering Our Place in the Web of Life — 9

    Chapter 2: The Plants Re-Member the People — 23

    Chapter 3: Weaving into the Wheel of the Year — 45

PART 2: The Herbal Wheel of the Year — 69

    Chapter 4: Spring — 71

        Nettle — 76

        Chickweed — 83

        Cleavers — 88

        Mugwort — 92

        Raspberry — 98

        Going Deeper into Spring — 102

    Chapter 5: Summer — 105

        Wild Rose — 112

        St. John's Wort — 118

        Yarrow — 124

        Calendula — 130

        Self-Heal — 134

        Going Deeper into Summer — 139

    Chapter 6: Fall — 143

        Devil's club — 149

        Huckleberry — 156

        Hawthorn — 161

        Rose Hips — 167

        Blue Elderberry — 170

        Going Deeper into Fall — 176

    Chapter 7: Winter — 177

        Red Cedar — 182

        Oregon Grape — 189

        Dandelion — 194

        Cottonwood — 199

Comfrey	205
Going Deeper into Winter	210

PART 3: *The Magic of Herbal Medicine-Making* 213

   Chapter 8: Making Medicine from the Bodies of Plants 215

   Chapter 9: Herbal Preparations 227

Infusions and Decoctions	232
Tinctures	235
Glycerites	238
Acetracts: Herbal Vinegars	239
Medicinal Syrups	240
Infused Oils	242
Herbal Salves	248
Herbal Baths	251
Flower Essences	253

   Chapter 10: Plants as Medicine 257

Conclusion: Toward a Re-Membered World 267

Glossary 273

End Notes 277

Appendix 280

   I: Home Herbal Aid Kit 280

   II: Resource List 282

Index 285

Author's Note 287

Artist's Note 289

Acknowledgments

I wish to thank the plant people, without whom we wouldn't be here, and the Mother Earth for the chance to live on her beautiful skin and to experience love. My great gratitude to all the folks who have shown up to my classes over the years, the gift of whose presence and attention allowed me to refine this work into something that made sense. Gratitude flows across the strands of time and space to the wisdom keepers, elders and ancestors who have kept the medicine of Earth-connection alive over the generations, despite all forces that have stood to stamp it out.

I am immensely grateful to wolf woman Lauren Blair Churchill for the beautiful artwork that gave image to these words; Renae Gilles for her expert wordsmithing and general book midwifery; Katy Pavlis for her timeless companionship and for dreaming deep and true; Tierney Salter for her trailblazing, inspiration and for the hands-on experience essential for slow cooking; Dancing Crow for her wise editing, spiritual generosity, and for being a precious living example; and the Olympic Mountains for weaving me into the deeper dreaming.

Finally, I wish to give thanks to my parents Karen and John for the gift of my life and their unconditional love; my husband David, who is the sanctuary of my heart, for the partnership that makes larger dreams possible; and my children Gwenna Rose and Callen John, whom I cherish beyond words, for making me a mother and for deepening my understanding of the purpose of life.

Introduction

By embarking on the adventure of learning herbalism, we are doing no less than reclaiming our original nature as people designed to be in kinship with the plants, who belong to Mother Earth, are dreamt by her dream, and serve the web of life from that place of remembrance. This book will reawaken that sense of Earth membership through the simple act of learning herbalism in alliance with the seasons while providing the necessary foundational knowledge to continue on a lifelong journey of herbalism.

This more traditional approach to herbalism could be defined as "allying with the plants to bring healing to the people." Orienting our herbal practices to the seasons, or the "wheel of the year," reminds us that we, like the plants who model it for us, are cycling and spiraling through the seasons along with the rest of nature. By tracking, understanding, and intentionally engaging with this seasonal rhythmic pulse, our connection to the Earth and her sacred cycles is deepened. Herbalism fosters a connection with these ancient wise green beings and it is they, the plants, that show us the way—season by season, year by year, cycle by cycle. The plants do nothing short of break us out of the spell of separation that dominates these modern times. In doing so, they initiate or deepen the process of reweaving us into full-fledged members of the web of life, members who remember their connection to the Dream of the Earth.

I have had the great privilege of setting hundreds of herbal-seekers on the lifelong road to strong relationships with the plants in my introductory seasonal, folk, and plant-spirit herbalism classes. The material herein has been shared and refined over years of teaching the "essential bones" of folk herbalism. It includes just enough yet not too much to overwhelm, enabling folks to get started on the herbal path. Herbalism is the medicine of the people. Every household should have access to this baseline folk knowledge.

Before diving right into the herbalism and getting our hands dirty, as herbalists love to do, it'd be wise to first understand the nature of the dirt we are diving into. Just as farmers cannot throw seeds into barren soil and expect them to simply grow, so too must we cultivate a fertile inner soil within our minds and hearts to plant the "simple" knowledge that comprises the study of herbalism. We begin our exploration by cultivating the backdrop, the right understanding, and the deeper meaning of why herbalism matters. We traverse the cosmology of an Earth-centered approach, exploring deeper layers of contact with the potential mysteries herbalism holds. On the surface, herbalism looks and seems simple. But with the proper soil and the right conditions, these simple seeds can grow into an old-growth forest like those of my Pacific Northwest home, nourishing life with their very existence. In this way, we are slow-cooked into heart- and soul-centered herbalists, serving and feeding life and future generations with our herbal efforts.

Practically speaking, a seasonal approach makes the study of herbalism feel more accessible, especially for beginners. By learning which plants to look for in spring, we can let go of and clear the mental space of all the other plants we are tracking. In spring we focus on spring, in summer we focus on summer, and so forth. Together we will move through the wheel of the year, traveling season by season, beginning with spring and ending with winter. Each season contains meditations, guiding questions, and teachings to help reweave us into an embodied remembrance of the seasonal spirit medicines as they move through the plants, us, and the web of life.

We explore the herbalism of each season, including what the plants' bodies are doing and what our considerations are as herbalists. Each season has detailed information on five medicinal plants, as I've found that five is a wise, reasonable, and robust number of plants to learn when we're first beginning our studies. The plants chosen are versatile and useful for home herbal care, either growing wild or easily found growing where people grow across most of North America. Just two of the plants, devil's club and red cedar, are specific to the West Coast. Information on how to harvest, process, and prepare each plant into medicine is shared, along with detailed and down-home useful descriptions of each plant's healing gifts. Formulas to stock the home medicine cabinet are sprinkled in along the way.

After our inner soil has been well cultivated, having met the seasons and the plants, we dive into the nuts and bolts of herbalism, exploring basic teachings, tools, resources, and practical knowledge that provide a steady enough foundation to begin practicing herbalism and really "doing the thing." We close by traversing the magical realm of herbal medicine-making, exploring recipes for creating tinctures, salves, syrups, and other basic formulas.

I have seen it happen over and over again. I've experienced it in my own bones. Seasonal herbalism works. It helps us learn the seasons, learn nature, learn the plants, learn herbalism, learn more of life and of ourselves. It brings us into closer contact with the plants as we remember how to ally with them to bring healing to the people in alignment with the Dream of the Earth and all of life.

Seasonal herbalism restores a memory of our place in the web of life and reignites a part of our humanity worth passing along to future generations.

May it be so for you, in service to all.

PART 1:
The Reweaving Power of Herbalism

"We must take our children to the wild, introduce them to the plants, and teach them of their connection to the Earth. In instilling in our children a respect for plant medicine, we not only care for their tender bodies but help pass along the seeds of a tradition that is as old as human life itself. We teach them to respect and care for the planet, for you cannot have a relationship with plants without entering fully into a relationship with Gaia, the living Earth."

— *Rosemary Gladstar,* <u>Rosemary Gladstar's Herbal Recipes for Vibrant Health</u>[1]

Chapter 1: Re-Membering Our Place in the Web of Life

"I believe that, seven generations beyond us, those who look back on our time will find that it was the cry of the trees that helped to restart the dreaming and foster the understanding that we must dream not only for ourselves but also for our communities and for all that shares life with us in our fragile bubble of air."

— *Robert Moss*, <u>Active Dreaming: Journeying beyond Self-Limitation to a Life of Wild Freedom</u>.[1]

Cultivating Fertile Inner Soil

What are we doing when practicing herbalism? The craft of herbalism, or "allying with the plants to bring healing to the people," requires much in the way of physical skills, such as wild harvesting, garbling, and medicine-making. It also requires the mental capacities of plant identification, memorization of medicinal actions, the ability to formulate and treat, and so forth. These physical and mental layers are essential for herbalism to "work" and are themselves profoundly healing for those versed in their craft. But at its best, herbalism penetrates much deeper—if we open up the channels within ourselves that understand what is happening beneath the surface. As the great Oglala-Lakota visionary Heȟáka Sápa, also known as Black Elk, said in his powerful testament *Black Elk Speaks*, "The power of a thing or an act is in the meaning and the understanding."[2]

One critical task of organic gardeners and farmers is to add as many nutritious ingredients to the dirt they tend as possible. These amendments help build a strong and varied soil matrix that provides just the right mix of nutrients, biodiversity, and fertility to receive the seeds planted by their hands. This fertile soil grows those seeds into food and medicine that feed the people and future generations.

It is the same with our minds and hearts. By adding many nutrient-rich amendments to our inner soil, we steadily cultivate a fertile garden bed into which we then plant the tiny unassuming seeds that are the nuts and bolts of herbalism. With luck and a bit of grace, when planted we are rendered fertile enough to grow those seeds into rooted and robust seasonal herbalists.

Living in Times of Repair

It's an exciting time to be alive. Exciting and also bewildering, heartbreaking, and confounding while simultaneously highly inspiring and creative. The name "Times of Repair" rings true. For something to be repaired, it has to have first been broken and I don't think anyone reading this book would argue that we aren't living in broken times. It is easy to fall into despair in the presence of so much breaking down. And yet there is hope. Even though the signs of destruction abound, so too does the regenerative power of the force of life.

I live on Washington state's Olympic Peninsula, an area known for its ancient old-growth forests. Anyone who visits the forest near my home remarks on how alive and magical the land feels. With deciduous alders and wild cherries as the dominant tree species, however, the land is clearly no longer in its original old growth. When visitors hear that the ancient forest was clear-cut for the second time in the 1990s, a sense of shock and disbelief bubbles through their spirits. Less than thirty years ago, this very same land that is now brimming with life, beauty, and holy vibrations, inspiring the heart of every person who sets foot on it, was decimated down to the skin of the Earth. This mass death was enacted with neither respect for life nor acceptance that living beings were being destroyed. This land could have withered away and retreated into lifeless despair, becoming a barren graveyard.

But this land didn't. The Earth herself doesn't. The plants don't and neither do you or I! We are resilient. By nature of our being here on this Earth, a regenerative healing capacity moves through us that is nothing short of miraculous.

Some seeds lie dormant for dozens, hundreds, or even thousands of years before deciding to sprout. What is the inspiration, impulse, or spark that initiates that rebirth? What do the plants know that we don't? Of one thing we can be sure: The plants know quite a bit more than we do, for they are literally our elders. Fossil records show that plants are hundreds of millions of years older than us humans, billions of years if we include the ocean plants before they migrated onto land. These photosynthesizing ancient ones have been here far longer than we have. In all ways, the plants predate and precede us, pioneering the way for life on Earth. It might be wise to look to these elders now for guidance.

The mission of modern human beings is to reweave our membership and belonging within the web of life. Our task is to feel, to sense, to know, to experience, to embody, and to remember that we are simply cells in the body of Mother Earth and that all creatures who share this Earth with us are our kin, no less than members of our family. It is from this remembering of our place in the order of things that our original nature might re-blossom, our original teachings from the Earth might be reintegrated, and a love for all of our kin on Earth might be reinstilled in our hearts.

How do we get there? How do we remember who we are, why we came here, and what our job is as human beings?

Plants are some of the teachers and role models that can guide us into the reweaving of an embodied remembrance within the web of life. Plants' bodies are still planted, literally rooted and plugged into the web of life. Learning herbalism, simple herbalism the way our ancestors did for millennia, restores our contact with those ancient deep-rooted elders. Herbalism is a part of the original design for humans living on this beautiful planet. It's the way of the past and it's the way of the future if the future is to include humans.

Being "Re-Membered"

Learning herbalism is an act of re-membering. Most of us think of the word "remember" as the retrieval of a memory or piece of cognition, of bringing something to mind. But the original meaning of this word holds a different and far deeper meaning. The word "remember" comes from the old Greek word "member," referring to an appendage or a limb. So to "re-member" is to reattach a limb or an appendage to its original place of belonging. In a re-membering process, the members, appendages, or limbs are being reattached to something they once belonged to.

Being re-membered is to be restored, returned, rehomed, re-wholed, rewoven, and reintegrated. Arms, a kind of limb or appendage, are not made to be separate from the human body. Arms belong attached to the core of the body as extensions of the heart's life-giving pulse. Arms are meant to create, serve, and protect the visions of the heart.

For us humans, to be re-membered is to come home to where we were made to be, to where we belong. We humans are members of this Earth. We are limbs, appendages, and members of the web of life. Our re-membering process is one of being consciously reintegrated into this web—of knowing, feeling, and experiencing in our cells, blood, and bones that we belong here. We are home here. All of the web of life is our kin.

Herbalism re-members us. Its introduction to the plant kingdom kicks off a reliable, natural, and sacred process of being re-membered by, reconnected to, and reattached to none other than the Earth herself. Interacting with the plants efficiently and effectively peels away the illusions of separation that cloud the modern mind, putting us smack-dab in the middle of knowing that we belong here, to this Earth. The study of herbalism heals the people. It re-members us.

We humans are akin to the arms in the web of life. What we remember in our re-membering is that our original design is to listen deeply to the pulse of the Earth's heartbeat, to create, serve, and protect the visions we receive from her vibrations—to create on behalf of, and to protect, all of life. Without our intending it, the plants will awaken an impulse toward Earth stewardship. Why? Because we inevitably end up falling head-over-heels in love with them. When we love them, we automatically long to protect them, for it is human nature to protect what we love. In loving the plants, we realize that their home is our home too. The plants and our love for them re-members us.

What Is Dreaming Us?

Those who wisely pay attention to such things have observed that in the past couple of decades, the images in children's dreams have shifted from natural symbols like plants and animals to more machine-like manmade materials.[3] Though it's not as common among modern people to believe so, dreams are as dream teacher Andrew Holecek describes them: the great truth-telling serum of the human psyche.[4] Dreams will tell it like it is, exactly how it is, even if we think we can fool ourselves into believing it's another way. The egoic veils that keep our mental realities comfy during the day are not available at nighttime as coping mechanisms. Dreams reveal the underlying substrate that is blossoming into the creation of waking-life reality.

The children's dreams tell us that, in no uncertain terms, Earth is ceasing to dream us. This is a powerful and disturbing revelation to ponder. Those who "dream the future" are no longer sourcing from something greater than themselves. We are increasingly dreamt by the consumerist, growth-centered, extractive, and very dominant "culture" that we all know we are stuck within and need to find our way out of. The dreams are being usurped, along with a future worth living for the children receiving these dreams. A painful truth.

This "culture" that is increasingly dreaming us wants us—needs us—to believe that "if we just know more, build more, create more, consume more . . . then, *then* we will be fixed. More, more, more, more, *more!*"

These are broken times, indeed.

As for myself though, I am a hopeful fool! As Dr. Clarissa Pinkola Estés says in her powerful and inspiring "Letter to a Young Activist During Troubled Times" essay, "I too have felt despair many times in my life, but I do not keep a chair for it. I will not entertain it. It is not allowed to eat from my plate."[5] So long as the Earth is still spinning, she is dreaming and if she is dreaming then we can hear her dreams and act accordingly. Night dreams are in fact one of the Earth's favorite ways of communicating with us.

A dear friend who is a powerful Earth dreamer was sent the following dream.

Katy's Dream: Avoiding the Watchtower
I am in a prison camp of some sort. It is entirely enclosed by a wire fence. It is not night or day, but a smokey haze illuminated by fire. I am being held here against my will with many other women. We are working together to try to escape. There is a giant watchtower that has an eye on top that ensures no one escapes. The eye is constantly turning and flashes a light over everything it scans. It is like a lighthouse but feels evil. Everywhere its light passes over, it sees. To escape the eye, I and the other women have to crawl on our

bellies, slithering like snakes on the dirt, along the perimeter of the fence until we find our way out.

Upon working with this dream in waking life, Katy received the following message: "To avoid the gaze of evil, stay close to the Earth." As she worked with the motif and the sensation of slithering like a snake on her belly across the Earth to escape the evil watchtower, a voice arose from within: "To avoid the gaze of evil, stay close to the Earth."

This dream has been one of the most important dreams "I" have ever "dreamt," though it did not enter through "my" dream door. Dreams are not meant for the dreamer alone. They long to be shared. In community dream work, there is a powerful practice of "dreaming the dream" of another. In this practice, we "try on the dream" of someone else and dream it as if it were our own dream. The dream of another becomes like a hat that we slip on over our own minds. The impressions and channels of energy that the dream opens within each individual's psyche become very real medicine for anyone given the chance to "dream the dream."

As I dream this dream, I hear the same words as Katy did arise from deep within: "To avoid the gaze of evil, stay close to the Earth." In my version of the dream, the voice feels as though it is from the Earth herself and further illuminations bloom in my psyche. Perhaps instead of looking up, out, and beyond, we should take a deep breath, sit down, look down, open our eyes, and see what, or in more respectful terms, *who* is right below and in front of us. Who is close to the Earth? The beautiful wise green beings who meet our gaze are still rooted in our mother the Earth, aligned with the holy force of nature as it pulses through the web of life. For too long, the plants have been waiting patiently for us modern ones to remember to simply look down, introduce ourselves, and say hello once again. They have much to teach us. They have not forgotten what it means to be here.

As I continue dreaming this dream, another channel of knowing opens up to flow inside of me. The evil of the watchtower in this dream is simply that which does not feed life. And that which does not feed life does not feed a future where there is life for the generations to come. Evil is that which is out of alignment with the flow of an abundant and generative good green Earth. It is that which has forgotten its original beauty and design. I feel a deep resonance of understanding inside me that gets it in my bones: This dream is teaching me how to feed life and to feed future generations.

Celebrated Nigerian philosopher Bayo Akamolafe is known for saying, "The times are urgent; let us slow down" as the salve to heal the breakdown surrounding us.[6] With all the chaos and urgency of the watchtower, these times are asking us to slow down, drop down, look down, and meet the plants we share the land with. They will introduce us to the animals, the elements, the seasons, and the dream of the very land where we reside.

Gaia and the Dream of the Earth

Scholar Thomas Berry gave the name "Dream of the Earth" to the holy force that is the interconnected web of life.[7] As people in today's world, we might be wise to focus our intentions and prayers on a plea to be reconnected to this

Dream of the Earth. To let the dreams of the Earth catch us, mold us, and reconnect us, to be blessed enough to remember the dreams we are sent and weave them into waking life on behalf of all things. This might, after all, be the original design for us humans. Numerous ancient land-based cultures, including the Celts of the British Isles and the Aboriginals of Australia, use the term "dreamers" to describe the people and their role in Creation.

The plants, by simply being, through their rootedness and belongingness, hook us into this Dream of the Earth. Their wild and wise ancient nature opens up channels within our own beings for the wild and wise ancient nature within us to flow. The plants help us become more receptive to these whisperings from the Dream of the Earth.

Perhaps before the dreams were usurped from nature, human beings were simply woven into an embodied connection with the Dream of the Earth. This connection wasn't even considered something noteworthy. It simply was an is-ness. It was the way of things. This Dream of the Earth informed people through their embodied experience, through their bodies' impulses, twitches, and instincts, through their emotional longings and desires, and through their dreams. The people, woven into the web of life, were in the flow, the rise and fall of the waves and contractions of the Earth herself pulsing through the people as through the rest of the web—one great organism cycling through time and space.

Somewhere deep inside of us, we can all feel something is off with the way things are and have been for many generations. For those of us whose ancestors left their indigenous lifeways in the more distant past, it can feel bewildering to know where to look for examples of Earth-honoring culture. Ancient Greece is one example of a Western civilization—a people who traded land-based living for empire—that still understood and culturally implemented an awareness of the aliveness of the Earth.

In the ancient Greek world, there was a sacred site known as Delphi, home of the famed Oracles of Delphi, holy priestesses who delivered prophecies to the people who traveled far and wide to seek their counsel. For millennia, the holy site at Delphi was considered sacred to the ancient Greek goddess Gaia, their name for Mother Earth. These oracles spoke on behalf of Gaia when giving their prophecies. They spoke for the Earth.

Let's take a moment to feel into this reality, imagining I am a farmer in the ancient Greek world. I make the long journey to visit the Oracles at Delphi for advice on building a new home for my family. The oracles respond on behalf of Mother Earth. Through them, Mother Earth foretells the ripple effects the clearing and construction of the new home will have upon the land's web of life if I choose my desired location. They prophesize that the project will impact my great-great-grandchildren's ability to farm the land. They see that the project will affect the animal populations and thus our ability to hunt and procure sufficient food. They share the opinions of the nature spirits who reside and govern the land, foretelling what their wrath might look like if the project is undertaken. They suggest that instead I consider rebuilding my home in a slightly different location. Through the oracles, Mother Earth shares that this new site will be less disruptive to the harmony of the land's web of life. The proper and necessary rituals to appease the nature spirits who will be displaced by the project are shared. I give great thanks to Mother Earth and to these holy women attuned to speak for her. I return to the land of my people to begin the necessary project in alignment with the Dream of the Earth.

This is the way it was at Delphi for millennia—women speaking for the Earth on behalf of all of life. Around 5,000 years ago, a shift occurred worldwide that marked the takeover of female gods by male gods. In other words, this was the dawn of the patriarchal era. At Delphi, the young male god Apollo arrived, wanting the power of the holy land and oracles for himself. To accomplish this feat, Apollo slew the great python who was the guardian protector of the site. With this slaying, Apollo usurped Gaia's throne at Delphi and the site became sacred to him. Moving forward, the priestesses no longer spoke on behalf of Gaia. They no longer spoke for Mother Earth and the web of life. They were now made to speak on behalf of the ambitious young male god Apollo. We can imagine how Apollo's prophecy might sound compared to Gaia's. It could be said that Apollo's voice still governs the direction in which people are marching today.

In modern times, the name Gaia Theory has been adopted to describe this consciousness of the Earth. The term, coined by chemist James Lovelock, posits that the Earth and its biological systems behave as a huge single entity.[8] Lovelock borrowed the term from the Greek tradition and its name for the deified Mother Earth, Gaia. This hypothesis is nothing new. In fact, some would argue it's as old as the Earth herself. For Earth-centered indigenous peoples all over the world, it was and is not a metaphor, symbolic, or just good manners to say "Mother Earth." It is quite literal.

If this Gaia Theory feels like a new concept, here is a metaphor that may be helpful. Let's imagine a human body, a body known as Leah. We can imagine how Leah is a constellation of trillions of cells all coalescing into this one organism known as Leah. There are various subsets of cells within Leah that are highly differentiated and specialized, such as nephrons, the functional units of the kidneys, and hepatocytes, the cells operating in the liver.

Let's imagine what the consciousness of each of those cells would be like in their own little micro-universes, experiencing themselves as separate and at the same time feeling a distant knowing that they are part of something greater. (Any of us who've ever experienced the haunting pull of an existential inner quandary or a full-on existential crisis know well the feeling described.) All of these cells are their own cell and at the same time they share a common home: Leah's body. And because these cells are part of Leah's body, they are connected to a higher intelligence, a life-preserving impulse that is constantly trying to seek homeostasis through up-regulating here or down-regulating there in service to the greater goal, which is Leah's continued life.

It is the same with Gaia. Truly! We are each of us, not just us human beings but every member of the web of life on this Earth, the cells of the body of Gaia. Each of us cells, by nature of our being here in this body of Gaia, are connected to the pulse of life, ever seeking to move her toward homeostasis.

Said another way, we are hooked by Gaia's dream, the dream of a future for herself.

At this particular time, we humans have gotten a bit out of balance, having forgotten how to do our job in the body of Mother Earth. We've forgotten our original purpose and have become sick, out of balance, metastatic even. And the entire system is suffering due to our forgetting.

Though we are indeed in a metastatic epoch, hope remains. Many of us have directly experienced, seen, or heard firsthand stories of healing miracles. We know that cells can change overnight and return to their healed and whole original design. Herbalism restores our contact with plants, themselves agents of miraculous healing. When we ingest them medicinally, plants open up pathways in our bodies for new healing energy to flow. This is how they heal our bodies. They do the same on the level of spirit, opening up pathways that pull us back into integration within the web of life, connecting us to the force of life and the possibility of miracles.

Chapter 2:
The Plants Re-Member the People

Belonging to Where We Are

We are all children of this Earth. We all belong here. And for many of us, the journeys of our ancestors carried them across the globe, leaving within our DNA the inheritance of a global history of movement and conquest. The downstream effect of this has led to a widespread sense of displacement and a feeling of un-belonging among many of us alive today as we are the recipients and bearers of these legacies. To halt the never-ending cycle of conquest, these times are asking us to be re-membered into belonging upon the land where we currently reside. The Earth is asking us to stop this unending movement and stay put, look at the land beneath our feet, and meet the beings who greet us right outside our front doors. These beings are none other than the wise green growing ones, our plant relatives. It is only after first arriving and inhabiting the place where we are that we can remember how we got here and decide who and how we'd like to be moving forward.

Life often requires us to move, to shift homes and change cities, and this movement is a natural part of the flow of life. If when we move we can be present *where we are* and make relations with the land and the plants there, we can begin to put a halt to the spread of the cultural pandemic of un-belonging. It's by keeping our feet close to the Earth where we are that our membership within the web of life can be re-membered. Fully being where we are is a powerful and, in these times, revolutionary act of putting a halt to the *more more more, move move move, next next next* consciousness that has wreaked havoc on the Earth and all her children, including us.

What this means for herbalists is a focus on building relationships with the plants that grow where we grow. Not where we will be next year when we just *get there get there get there* or even where we were before, but exactly where we are right now in this current moment.

There are many reasons for this suggestion. One very practical reason is that local herbal medicine acts powerfully on the bodies of local people. The plants we share a sliver of Mother Earth with are under the same influences elementally, ecologically, and climatically as we are. They are made from the same stuff and substrate as us. This makes their bodies just the right agents of healing to help our bodies attune to the influences of our unique shared bioregion. The bodies of local plants often manufacture perfectly crafted cocktails of biochemical constituents to help our bodies weather the storms of the stressors that life in our shared bioregion offers. For example, in the Pacific Northwest, ingesting the bodies of red cedar leaves and Oregon grape roots often has just the right mix of antimicrobial, decongestant, and immune-boosting molecules that help the lungs and immune systems of the people facing the damp, congesting conditions of our shared climate.

Another reason for working with local plants is accessibility. If we know how to work with the plants that grow where we grow, then we are not asking the energy of fossil fuels and other agents of global commerce to provide our medicine, lightening the load on the web of life. Sustainability naturally arises from focusing our herbalism on the plants who are our neighbors.

More subtle yet just as powerful is that getting to know the plants who grow where we grow nurtures our relationship with the land beneath our feet. This reweaving into the ground that holds us restores our sense of belonging and reawakens an embodied knowing of our kinship with all of life. When this kinship is directly experienced, it awakens an authentic desire to serve, protect, and steward the land that we share. The plants reweave us into the local web of life, pulling us deeper into a conscious embodiment of this truth.

Plants as Spiritual Masters

Plants are pure emanations of divine energy and as such can serve as mirrors, teachers, and healers, all of which are different aspects of the same thing. Unlike humans, plants have not forgotten their divine nature and interbeing-ness with all things. After all, their bodies are still plugged into the great web of life. Engaging with a plant is very similar to what in the Vedic tradition of India is called "guru meditation," a practice involving deep contemplation of a guru, saint, or deity. By meditating on the holy person, we learn about the qualities they possess. Over time, those qualities are awakened in our own beings and eventually true inner healing and transformation blossom from that awakening. We become like that holy person. Our own guru nature awakens. The plants offer the same inspiration as the gurus. As we humans navigate our challenges, our forgettings, and our dis-eases, the plants serve to reflect back to us the divine energy that informs them, rooted into the web of life as they are. In so doing, they invigorate and strengthen the flow of that very same divine energy within us.

Let's imagine a circumstance where it feels as though life has betrayed us too many times and there has been simply more heartbreak than we can handle. We might be struggling to keep our hearts open to life, our heart energy and sense of hope having all but shut down. Perhaps we have even begun to experience cardiovascular symptoms like high blood pressure and chest pains. At this juncture, which might even be experienced as a crisis, we can call on the tutelage and healing presence of rose, a plant whose energy holds the template of pure divine love. As we invite rose in, she teaches us about herself, eventually reflecting back that we too have the template for divine love within our own hearts. Rose shows us that our thorns are actually a part of our divine beauty, that our betrayals have served to soften us and wisen us to when and how to set proper boundaries. By being touched by rose's medicine, our hearts slowly begin to reopen to the flow of life and to the potential of love. When this flow is restored and reawakened, our healing is well underway.

The encounter with rose that precipitates healing might occur in any number of ways. The invitation is simply to bring the energy of a plant teacher into the spheres of our lives, homes, and hearts. We might drink rose petal tea. We might bathe in a tea of rose petals. We might spend time in nature meditating at the feet of a rose bush. Just like sitting in communion with a spiritual master or holy being, we can be touched by the divine healing energy of plants in any number of ways. Our job is to invite them in and then keep our hearts and minds open and receptive, allowing their energy to enter, teach, and transform us.

Holding Holism in Mind

We likely all agree that a human being is something more than the total function of their anatomical and physiological structures, that there is an essence to a person that is greater and holier than just the sum of their physical parts. The very same is true of plants. Far more than the sum total of their biochemical constituents, each plant is a grand being with a unique essence that cannot be adequately summarized by merely dissecting their anatomy or physiology.

As herbalists, we train ourselves to see people with "holistic eyes," a gaze that enables us to see the interconnection of all things. With holistic eyes, we see that rather than being dissected and analyzed simply according to physical symptoms, our physical health exists in relation to all aspects of life. We know that to truly understand a person, we must tune into their personality, personal and ancestral history, what their environment is like, the composition of their family and social networks, the dreams they have at night, the secret wishes they hold for their lives, the gifts and talents they possess, the struggles they have faced and overcome, and so much more.

This holistic gaze that herbalists develop for people should also fall upon the plants we are working with as we strive to see them as vastly intricate beings. Plants do contain these chemical constituents that, by some miracle, have medicinal effects on human bodies. This is nothing short of amazing. And the plants are much more.

In our herbalism studies, it'd be wise to train ourselves to track and learn both the physical and spiritual energies of the plants we study. The physical aspects include the effect the body of a plant has on the body of a person—the list of medicinal action terms, constituent profiles, and physical tissue states that the plant can help restore and harmonize. The spiritual aspects include a plant's essence and divine architecture—the unique tune of Creation they are and emulate. Our knowledge of their spiritual energies may be informed by teachings the plants share with us directly; impressions we receive from dreams, meditations, or plant journeys; as well as elemental or celestial correspondences. If we maintain that holistic gaze, holding both the physical and the spiritual throughout our journey with herbalism, we will bring our practice to the level of spirit and soul. When we see the plants, the people, and all of life in this way, then we are truly living, serving, and healing at the level of the soul.

Our Ancestors Were Herbalists

Our ancestors were herbalists. Each of us has to go back different amounts of time. For some of us, it's millennia and for others, it never turned off. But in the DNA of our beings, there is an epigenetic seed lying dormant. Patiently waiting over many generations, the ancient spark in this ancestral seed knows that "allying with the plants to bring healing to the people" is the natural way of things. There is always a deep sense of rightness, homecoming, and reclaiming that enters the soulsphere when one embarks on the path of herbalism. It's a homecoming of no less than pieces of the ancestral soul, indigenous to all of us.

Herbalism has always been the medicine of the people. The plants belong to none save the Earth herself and they are incredibly generous. People have always and everywhere had access to their gifts of nourishment and medicine. It's only in very recent history that capitalistic and scientific efforts have been undertaken to own, control, and manipulate the sacred design of plants. As science and capitalism have grabbed hold of herbalism, it has had the devastating effect of taking herbalism out of the hands of the people. One reason for this is simple accessibility. It's a downright privilege to live in an area with access to wild spaces, let alone to have the square footage for a garden or a few pots. Capitalism has tied profits to plants in the form of the herbal industry, making herbal medicines inaccessible to people below a certain economic level.

Most devastating of all is that the people no longer *believe* that herbalism is *their* medicine. Mainstream integration has served to cut most people off from a simple belief in the healing gifts of the plants. Even the privileged few who do have financial access to plant medicines no longer *believe* it's *their* medicine. These folks often see all the herb books available, see the hundreds of tincture bottles in supplement stores, and hear experts pontificating on the herbal research being done. All of this makes herbalism seem intimidating and out of reach. Many unknowingly adopt the belief that herbalism is too advanced or somehow beyond them.

Herbal knowledge is the birthright of all people and it is only very recently that this has changed. As long as there are plants growing from the ground, herbalism is still here for the people. We don't need to be gifted in math, biochemistry, or pathophysiology to harvest plants. We don't need to be literate, let alone scientifically literate, to make medicines to keep ourselves, our families, and our communities well. This is an ability we all have and until very recently, every household held this baseline herbal knowledge. Every family knew how to gather herbs, make medicines, and support itself through most bumps along the road of life.

We need to return to "folk herbalism," an herbalism that is accessible to the people, simple enough that most everyone can understand it. Herbalism is meant to feel and be within our reach, instead of off in a distant ivory tower. The medicine-making instructions and recipes shared in this book utilize what has become known by modern herbalists as the "folk method." It is a way of making medicine that involves minimal math and no need for an understanding of biochemical constituents. The folk method is simple and it is effective. It's the way our ancestors were making medicine for millennia in their own hearths and homes to keep their families and communities well, all around the world.

Building Relationships with Plants

As master herbalist Svevo Brooks said, "My idea of a good herbalist isn't someone who knows the uses of forty different herbs, but someone who knows how to use one herb in forty different ways."[1] Though it can be hard for the ravenous beginner's mind to accept, there is indeed great wisdom in this statement. It's important to remember this notion as we continue to dip our toes into the world of herbalism and it is why this book focuses on only five plants each season. With so much information available to us online and in books, it can be very easy to fall into the trappings of overwhelm, thinking we need to learn it all in order to "count" as herbalists. From experience, I've learned the wisdom of starting small on an herbal learning journey, trusting that knowledge will build over time. The beginning years of study are really about "learning how to learn" herbalism. Remember, the plants are the teachers and the healers. Our job as herbalists-in-training is to ally with them, which means to simply get to know them. It is the fruits of these alliances that bring healing to the people.

Everything of substance in Creation derives from *relationships.* The deeper the relationship one has with a plant, the more they function as a human ambassador or channel of that plant's healing energy. Said another way, the deeper one's relationship with a plant, the more that plant's divine energy has been awakened and turned on inside of them—the more *they are the plant.* Just like in relationships with people, relationships with plants require time, commitment, effort, and dedication.

Herbalism is a walk of *wisdom,* not merely a walk of *knowledge.* But wisdom is something we must be slowly cooked into. The path of the wise herbalist takes time to unfold as deep relationships do not happen overnight, over the course of a one-weekend workshop, or even a two-year degree program. It takes much effort and time spent with the plants for a deeply felt sense of relationship to sprout. It takes time for assimilation and integration to occur. We have to be cooked into our cellular understanding.

Herbalism takes time to begin to work its reweaving magic. As we begin our journey, we can rest assured that there is much happening beneath the surface of our awareness, just like there is under the soil of our beloved plants. If disillusionment or overwhelm creep into the mental room, we can simply disinvite them, reassuring ourselves that our foundation is being set, relationships are building, and we are well on our way to the "click" feeling of embodied knowing.

In the meantime, how might we go about allying with and getting to know these wise green elders? A good entry into that question is to consider how we go about getting to know another person. If there is a new someone we admire and would like to get to know, how might we enter into a courtship with that potential friend? We might call them up, visit their home, invite them to ours, share meals, share tea, ask them questions, bring gifts, exchange stories, and more. In essence, we dedicate our time and energy to them, feeding the blossoming relationship with the gift of our intention and attention.

It is the very same for the plants we are hoping to ally with. By seeing the plants as our kin, elders, potential healers, teachers, and lifelong friends, we can find our way into courting them. Here are some ideas for ways of getting to know and building relationships with the plants.

Sit with a plant and breathe. As we sit in this whole cycle of spirit, breathing in and out, we understand in an embodied manner that we and the plants are so intricately entwined in this web of life that we quite literally *create each other's breath*. How could we not be related?

Visit the plants in their homes. Find them in the wild. If we are less familiar with our local ecology, the act of "plant hunting" might take longer, but the hunt will foster familiarity with our local land. Once the plants are found in their homes (hooray!) we can look around and notice: What is the land like? Is the land wet or dry? Is it a forest, meadow, or disturbed area? Who are this plant's friends? Who do they like to grow near? All of these noticings begin to teach us about their spirit medicine and deepen our understanding of the plant's essential nature.

Invite the plants into our homes. Plant them in the garden if we have one. The act of caring for and stewarding a plant puts us in a direct relationship with them. In tending to their growing, we learn what kind of soil they like, how much water they thrive in, and who they like to grow near as well as their life cycle and what their bodies look like throughout the year. All of this hints at their deeper medicinal gifts.

Ask the plants about themselves and listen deeply to their responses. Sit down, close the eyes, invite the heart to open, and draw awareness to the space of interbeing between a plant and ourselves. Once this heart connection is made, we can ask the plant to show us what the medicine is that they carry. Trust whatever feelings, knowings, thoughts, memories, and sensations arise during this exchange. These are the plant's answers to our inquiries. Just because the plants don't have voice boxes with which to speak does not mean they are not communicating. This skill of deep listening to other-than-human life forms is transferable and an important competency of Earth membership and belonging. Keep practicing. As with anything, it will feel more natural the more we practice.

Share about ourselves with the plants. We can tell them our stories, sing them songs, and share our woes, griefs, troubles, and confusions, as well as our triumphs, successes, and longings. We can share from the heart, being vulnerable, authentic, and real. As in any relationship of substance, we must reveal our true natures in order for real intimacy to blossom.

Draw or paint the plants. Art automatically shifts us into a right-brain state of consciousness, putting us in a more receptive state to engage in communication with our nonhuman kin. The act of focusing on painting or drawing the plants' bodies helps us really see them more deeply and understand the intricacies of their forms. It nurtures the blossoming relationship between their spirits and our own. It also helps us learn their bodily structure, which then aids our competency in plant identification.

Make plant pressings. Plant pressings are an easy and beautiful way to bring the energy, beauty, and bodies of the plants into our homes and thus into our psychic spheres. Simply place a plant's body flat between two sheets of paper and stack heavy books on top. When the plant is dry and flat, craft glue can be used to stick them to acid-free paper. Pop them in a frame and voilà! The plant is a member of our home.

Have a cup of tea with a plant. This is a beautiful ritual. We can make a cup of tea from the plant we are getting to know. One teaspoon of fresh or dried plant material per cup of water steeped for 15 minutes is a general rule. Sip that tea while engaging in a heart-centered dialogue. Notice what happens to the body, mind, emotions, and spirit when the plant's body is brought into our own. Of course, we shouldn't ingest any plants whose identity we are not certain about; see the section on herbal safety on page 60.

Read about the plants. Learn what our fellow humans have learned from the plants by reading their books and writings. You do not need hundreds and hundreds of herb books, just a solid handful that you resonate with that inform your particular walk with herbalism. Learning practical knowledge about a plant grounds our more intuitive knowings into a dynamic duo of holistic herbal wisdom. Every wise herbalist has both knowledge and intuition in equal parts to inform, inspire, and dance with one another in a beautiful harmony.

Meditate with the plants. We can meditate with a plant either by holding its body in the hands, sipping tea, taking a few drops of tincture or essence, or by sitting in communion in the wild. We can commune in this way in silence or by playing a shamanic drumbeat track to help shift the mind into a more receptive, nonlinear state. This meditation truly becomes a heart communion where we deepen into a state of being with a plant.

Make the plants into medicine. An entire section of this book is dedicated to the art and science of medicine-making. Garbling, processing, medicine-making, and then ingesting these preparations is a sacred alchemy that we enter into with plants. We ingest the plants, in forms lovingly curated by our own hands in a sacred manner, to feed our own life energy.

Carry a plant in a medicine bag. All that is necessary is a small pinch of a plant's body in order to keep its energy close to our own. Carry a bit of a plant's body on your person in a medicine bag, a piece of jewelry, or tucked into a pocket. This proximity helps attune our consciousness to the consciousness of the plant, helping to integrate its medicine into our own beings.

Leave offerings for the plants. Offerings can be as diverse as the people who offer them and there are no rules other than that the gift should come from the heart. Make offerings from plants grown in the garden or wildcrafted by hand and infuse them with prayers and blessings. Keep these blends in a special pouch worn around the neck or tucked into a harvest basket when out in the wild or in the garden.

Make art with the plant's body. Sacred crafting is a beautiful way to bring the healing gifts of the plants into one's life. Create jewelry with their bodies, put pieces of the plants inside of rattles, or craft medicine items of all kinds. The only limit is one's creativity and ingenuity.

Save and share their seeds. Share your love of these plants with others and teach them how to grow and care for them. Spread the love. Serve and protect the plants' future generations as well as your own. Plant the future.

Find out how to help protect the plants' habitats and future generations. Get involved with local stewardship and protection and become aware of the needs plants have for their particular ecosystems. United Plant Savers is an amazing organization dedicated to planting and protecting future populations of medicinal plants.[3]

Dream with the plants. This is a personal favorite, learned from my first herbal teacher, Molly. Once certain of the identity and safety of a plant, place a freshly harvested sprig in a glass of water by the bed. Set the intention to dream with the plant during the night and drink the glass of water first thing upon awakening. Record any dreams or images that came during the night. If we're lucky enough, the plant's spirit might visit in a manner that we remember. Consider keeping a special journal only for these plant dreams.

Dreaming

Dreaming is a powerful and important skill for conscious members of the web of life. If we are able to unclog and open our dream doors, we provide a clear path for the wisdom, healing, and relationship from the plant spirits to more readily flow.

The dreams that knock at night are nothing less than messages from the divine—the Otherworld on the other side of the veil as my Celtic ancestors called the dream world(s). Most of us place little to no importance on dreams, while the opposite is true for all Earth-centered cultures. The land where we live, the animal spirits, the ancestors, and Mother Earth herself all communicate with us through our nighttime dreams. The plants generously visit, teach, and heal us at night, regularly showing up at the dream doors of those of us who are interested. For these reasons alone, though there are many others, making an effort toward reclaiming our nighttime dreams and growing our skill in making meaning of them are very worthwhile re-membering endeavors.

Perhaps you, like many in the modern world, have lost your dreams or, rather, your dreams have lost you. In a dominant culture that pays them little attention, it is no surprise that the dreams take a hiatus, moving on to more interesting and interested places. There is no doubt that we live in a dream-impoverished time. But thankfully, like all of Creation, our dreams respond to our attention, our intention, our adoration, and our love. If you are one who would like to reclaim your inner dreamer and improve your ability to catch them, here is a recipe for turning the dreams back on. I call it "Personal Dream Practice 101."

Dream Altar — Have a dream altar next to the bed or a dream image or item on a larger personal altar. An altar is a landing pad or embodied affirmation of the energies we are aligning with, the intentions we are setting and calling into our lives. By making an altar, we are asserting to the forces of dreaming and life who we are and what we are standing for. On the altar, place any items that feel as though they represent the inner dreamer. A few options include dried mugwort, an image of the Moon, a stone or crystal ball such as moonstone or quartz, a picture of Artemis or another dreaming goddess, or a bowl of water. This simple yet powerful dream altar practice is a declaration to the universe, "Hello out there! Just so you know, I am a dreamer! Send me more dreams, please!"

Intention — Set the intention before bed, "I will have beautiful dreams and remember them," as though it's a mantra or affirmation and repeat these words many times in your mind at night while falling asleep. For those who are more prayerful, praying might feel more juicy than an affirmation. Both affirmation and prayer are equally fine and depend on our authentic relationship with Spirit and life. If praying, call out to whatever higher guidance you find home within, ask for help in expanding the dreams, and share the hope to have more dreams and to remember them. Do this each night while going to sleep.

Record — This is by far the most essential step to take in expanding one's dreams. We must have a way to "catch" the dreams we receive before they slip back across the threshold to remain forever in the dream world. Keep a dream journal or audio recording device next to your bed and first thing upon awakening, record anything and everything you remember. The dreams need not be in complete sentences or finished thoughts. In fact, the more "raw" a state they are in, the purer "dream speak" they are. Some people find it easier to audio record dreams on their phone and this is great too. Figure out the way of recording that works with your life and personality flow and then do it every single morning.

Gratitude — Each morning upon awakening, either in bed before rising or during morning spiritual practices, add a little "clause/pause" in the routine to honor and thank the dreams. Take the time to honestly and heartfully send gratitude and thanks to the source of dreams each morning: "Thank you for dreaming me. I am listening. I am here. Thank you." As the magical force of gratitude does, this little time and step magnifies the energies of the dreaming, encouraging our dream source to keep it up.

Associate — Your dreams are a conversation between you and your higher self, the part of your expanded self that makes and dreams you. The symbols that are spun and sent through the dream door are the absolutely perfect clothes that the energies or messages wear to come, get your attention, and wake you up. Our humble little job as the humans down here on Earth is to figure out what the symbols and messages mean. The process of trying to figure this out is often called "making associations." The practice goes like this: In a journal, write down the dream symbol or image, then allow the mind and hand to "free write" or "automatic write" what comes to mind in the presence of this symbol or image from the dream. These associations come from the unconscious and begin to open up and bloom the deeper meanings of the symbols.

"Aha" — After having made associations via free writing, reread the dream with the associations in mind and closely track your body to observe for an "Aha" to arise. These are clues as to the dream's deeper meanings. There are many words for the "click" feeling of embodied knowing, of truth having been told. Goosebumps are a pretty universal and well-known experience of the Aha. The Aha can also feel like a heart opening, a flood of energy, full body tingles, spontaneous crying, or like a punch to the gut of a painful truth having been spoken. Our bodies tell us when they are in the presence of truth and it is often contrary to what the mind believes or wants to believe.

Meaning — After making associations and noticing any Ahas, revelations, or insights that have arisen, next seek to harvest some meaning from the dream. These questions can be helpful: If this dream did come in service to my health and wholeness (which I can assure you, it did), what is its message? What is its medicine? I sometimes like to call this step the "medicine mantra" of a dream. Free-write the medicine mantra of the dream while holding the expanded energy freed from the association and Aha processes.

For example, in a recent dream of mine an older woman I know and love well was in the process of dying and was being assisted by a great holy woman in her dying process. The dream took place in my old childhood home and members of my family of origin were also present. After making associations with each figure in the dream and listening closely to my body's response, I asked the dream for its medicine mantra. The answer that spontaneously arose, "Don't fear that which is falling away, for it's held in the arms of holiness," is of course quite applicable to my current waking life and elicits shivers of Aha. This is great feedback that I'm on the right track to harvesting the meaning from this dream.

Act — Having made some applicable, relevant meaning from the dream, it's now time for the "weaving" part of "dreamweaving." We have to *weave* the freed energies from the dream into our waking lives. If we fail to *do* something with the dream's messages, then the dream's potential is lost, its energy falls flat, and transformation is halted. Action steps or rituals to weave the dream energies can look any number of ways. The important thing is to do something to ground and incarnate the dream energies. Here are some ideas, though this is just the tip of the iceberg.

* Write down the medicine mantra from the dream and stick it on your altar, bathroom mirror, car dashboard, or somewhere you will see it regularly.
* If you dreamt of a person, place, or thing, seek out that person, place, or thing in waking life. The more often we can "walk the literal dream" in this waking world, the more powerfully we blend the dream world with this one. If you dreamt of a red dress, wear the red dress. If you dreamt of a beaded necklace, make the beaded necklace.
* Do more research. If you dreamt of an animal, a goddess, a place, or a name, research that symbol and continue researching until you find any Ahas that alert you that you're on the right track.
* Take the dream material to a therapist, healer, teacher, or mentor to honor, ground, and further nurture what arose in the dreamscape into becoming.
* Make art of the dream. Paint the symbol, character, or figure from the dream. This quite literally weaves, or births, the dream energies into waking life, giving them a very physical form in this world.

Plant Dreams

The plants will visit the dream doors of those who are interested and paying attention and when this happens it is indeed a great blessing. When the plants bring teachings in the dreams, it is wise to honor the visitation by visiting and leaving an offering of gratitude to the plants or by sending gratitude in our prayers and spiritual practice. It is also wise to document any teachings the plants share so that they are remembered when the time comes when they are needed. I find the healing that flows from the implementation of dream plant medicine is often stronger, more soulful, and more lasting than ordinary knowledge. So much so that when I am gifted plant teachings in dreamtime, I treat them like treasures of gold from the divine, writing down every word and tidbit so I don't forget the gift.

Here is a lovely example of a dream teaching, healing, and ceremony gifted to me in the dreamtime by the wise and noble rosemary.

At the time I received the dream, in waking life I was dealing with a very overwhelming situation, the intensity and toxicity of which was plaguing my mind, mood, and outlook. It was very mentally heavy. In the dream, a wise medicine woman elder instructed me to wash my hair with rosemary, showing me how to make a strong tea from the rosemary and pour it over my hair and head. This little ritual, the wise woman showed me, would spiritually wash the residue of the situation from my mind. Still in the dream, I found a bundle of rosemary sprigs with a little label tied around it. The label had the words "Love Grows Here" written on it. I knew that this was rosemary and the wise woman's way of teaching me that the hair-washing ritual would not only cleanse my mind but also plant the reminder seeds that "love grows here." This ritual would return my mind to love, a spiritual healing gift of rosemary I was unaware of.

Upon awakening from this dream, I immediately gave great thanks, knowing that an authentic visitation had occurred. I found a place where rosemary grows and brought an offering to the plant, leaving it with a prayer of heartfelt gratitude for visiting me in my dreams, for sharing the teaching with me, and for gifting me the healing ceremony. I asked and was granted permission by the plant to harvest a few sprigs to enact the ceremony. I did the "Rosemary Love Grows Here" ceremony and I'm happy to report that I was able to successfully untangle my mind from that toxicity. Since the dream, I've shared this ceremony with others plagued by inner turmoil and inner or outer mental toxicity, those who needed the reminder to grow love in their minds, all thanks to rosemary and one little dream.

Chapter 3:
Weaving into the Wheel of the Year

The following meditation with the Earth helps to ground an embodied sense of the wheel of the year and of our interconnection with the seasonal forces. This practice, when done regularly, helps to deepen relationships with the spirit medicine of the seasons and deepens our alignment with the rhythms of the Earth as she spirals through her cycles. Said another way, this practice reweaves us into the Dream of the Earth.

Find a spot in nature that calls to you where there is plenty of plant life to commune with and to reflect the seasonal energies. For example, if it's spring, choose a spot where baby sprouts are popping up from the ground or recently burst leaf buds are adorning the shrubs and trees. If it's fall, you might tuck into a nest of fallen leaves on the Earth.

Once you and your spot have found each other, take the time to connect into this place. Invite your root, the area beneath and around your sitz bones, to soften. Open and invite the energy of Mother Earth to rise and meet you. Invite your heart space to open and as you do, invite the energy of Mother Earth to join you in your heart space. Take the amount of time necessary to establish this connection. Once it is made and you and the Earth can really feel each other, heartfully ask her to help show you, remind you, re-member, and reweave you into a felt sense of your interconnection with all of life, all her children, all your kin.

Notice what arises after having made this inquiry and follow its threads, lingering in this space for as many minutes as it takes to experience a felt sense of interconnection beginning to occur. Open up your field of awareness to include the web of life that exists beneath the entire soil layer, or skin, of Mother Earth. Underneath this soil is a vast interconnected system of mycelium, animals and their burrows, creepy crawlies, roots and rootlets, and all other manner of life. Connect as deeply and as widely with this web of life as you can and feel that you too are a part of it.

Next, open your eyes and look around, seeing with the eyes of your heart the plant life that surrounds you. These relatives, these green elders, are reflections of the wild Dream of the Earth as it is also pulsing through you right here and right now. What the plants' bodies are doing—whether they are budding, blossoming, withering, or otherwise—is a true reflection of what is occurring within your spirit.

Allow yourself to come into resonance with the plants, allowing them to awaken in you a deeper experience of your belonging to the Earth and all of life. Allow their reflection to open channels within you where the seasonal spirit medicine can flow, showing you how to walk in alignment with the Dream of the Earth through her seasonal march.

Allow the knowings, understandings, and cellular re-memberings to work their way into your psyche, heart, and soul. Continue until you really fully feel the season's spirit within you and all around you—the season that is upon the Earth and the season that you are also within by being a member of her web of life. Breathe into that membership within the web of life as you allow the season to vibrate throughout your cells.

From this place of connection, reflect upon the following.

* What does it mean to be a member of the web of life?
* What are the duties and responsibilities that arise from my membership?
* What is the Dream of the Earth for herself? What is my role in this Great Dream?

It's wise to repeat this meditation as often as we're able, so much so that eventually every step we take upon the Earth becomes an available opportunity to be reminded of our kinship, our belonging, and our interconnection to the plants and all of life.

When out in nature, make a practice of cultivating a heart connection between self and all other members of nature. Plants and nature communicate more subtly. They are not overt and loud like we humans. Instead, communications happen on a quieter level, through the heart. Notice how the heart and entire being shift when in the presence of other beings in nature. A change in emotions or sensations or even spontaneous memories arising can all indicate a connection has been made. The communication becomes easier to discern with practice and awareness. When practiced regularly, moving through the world in this manner will over time begin to become an is-ness again.

For those who find this meditation or others like it difficult to access, do not fear or deem yourself a failure. Most of us have an amount of atrophy in our ability to access states of consciousness where our interconnection with all of life occurs. Beginners especially are often stumped by the suggestion that the Earth and plants can talk, wondering how we could communicate with beings who don't speak the same way we do. Others know that interspecies communication is *a thing*, yet doubt their ability to engage in the interaction.

Because these ways of connecting are not valued by the dominant culture, the modern psyche tends toward a diminished capacity in the nonlinear, creative, and holistic capacities of the brain and instead tends to do linear, rational, and intellectual consciousness quite well. It has been my experience that with practice these latent capacities can be awakened and restrengthened.

Regularly listening to shamanic drumbeats in a frequency range of 4 to 7 Hz is a wonderful training program for cultivating capacity in the right-brained expansive state. This right brain is the part of our neurology that engages in communication with other-than-human realms, the place where holism reigns, and where we experience the interconnectedness of all things. Find a good shamanic drumbeat recording and make a practice of listening to it regularly. During the drumming, imagine having a conversation with a plant. Imagination is the doorway to spirit, so simply follow the imagination's flow. The more we practice traversing the imaginal, the more our consciousness easily shifts into this expansive state. As with all things, it simply requires practice. The more we engage in these modes of consciousness, the more grounded, integrated, and embodied our capacity becomes.

Cycling with the Seasons

A fact of life on this beautiful Earth is that she is constantly in motion, cycling through the seasons. Various places of her body, what we call "locations," experience these seasons and this spiraling cyclical rhythm in different ways. Because we are of the Earth and in a real sense *are* the Earth, we too are cycling through these seasons, these ebbs and flows. The modern way of human life might shelter us from this truth in various degrees through things like air conditioning and modern heating. But the fact remains: We are of this Earth and affected by her cycles. The seasonal shifts are happening on the internal, even if we can pretend they are not on the external.

As the Earth cycles through the seasons, all of life cycles with her, including our bodies and the bodies of plants. The plants' bodies demonstrate the seasonal shifts more clearly than our bodies and we can look to them to pull us deeper into the seasonal rhythm.

For plants, the seasonal dance is marked by the following general growth pattern.

* First, **seeds** sprout from the soils of the Earth.
* Next, **leaves** form, whose purpose is to photosynthesize and obtain nutrients from sunlight.
* Then, **flowers** arrive to improve the plants' chances of reproduction.
* Finally, the **fruits** form, facilitating seed dispersal for future reproduction.

* After seed dispersal, an annual plant completes its life cycle and returns to the Earth. Unless they are evergreen, perennial plants consolidate their resources into their **roots**, turning toward life underground.

There are correspondences to human bodies at each of these stops upon the wheel of the year. As spring arrives, the baby nettles poke out and the deciduous tree buds begin to swell, reflecting what is happening within our human bodies. We too are emerging from the winter of our own beings, having retreated within to gestate the next cycle of self-growth. As we ponder this reflection, we are re-membered by what it means to let the decay go, that last year's growth is now the compost of this year's sprouting. Hope permeates the atmosphere as we remember that we too can be reborn anew, nurtured by the freshly composted decay of the past.

This coherence with the rhythm of nature is true on the level of energy and spirit and it's true on the physical. Ingesting medicinal and edible plants throughout the year as nature makes them available helps align our physical bodies with nature's rhythms. For example, eating bitter young shoots and leaves in spring when they are available helps cleanse the body and blood, restoring vitality and light to the system. This decreases the likelihood of seasonal allergies, boosting the immune system and increasing overall energy levels. The physical support restores the spiritual vigor needed to plant our dream seeds, and literal seeds, during the year to come.

When late spring and early summer arrive, the plants' bodies are making flowers. Interacting with these flowers mirrors the radiant beauty of our own self-expression, reminding us that it's good to be alive. The exquisite sight and divine smells settle and soothe our nervous systems, allowing us to open into an embrace of our sensual natures. The flowers teach us to settle into being the beauty that nature needs us to be.

In fall and winter, nature provides our bellies and souls with the roots of plants. As we dig roots and reflect upon their nature, we are reminded of what it means to go within, to reserve our energies, and to drop down to what really matters. The closeness of death reminds us of the preciousness of life and we are grateful for the roots that keep us nourished and cleansed throughout the winter.

Throughout the wheel of the year, the plants serve as teachers and mirrors of how to align with the Earth, her rhythms and her cycles, constantly reminding us that we too are members of the web of life. In this dance of relationship, we are rewoven.

The Seasonal Herbal Dance

Just like their human relatives, plants are composed of many body parts, big and small. The six major parts of plants' bodies are roots, stems, leaves, fruits, flowers, and seeds. Perennials are plants whose bodies live for many years and put energy toward growing roots underground. Annuals are plants whose bodies only live for one turn of the wheel and don't put as much energy toward root growth.

Each plant has a particular part of its body that houses its highest medicinal constituents. These are referred to as plant parts. For example, an apothecary label for stinging nettle might read "stinging nettle leaf," whereas skullcap would read "skullcap aerial parts," etc.

- Medicinal **leaves** include nettle, lemon balm, and many members of the mint family.
- Medicinal **flowers** include rose, St. John's wort, yarrow, calendula, lavender, and chamomile.
- Medicinal **fruits** include hawthorn berry, juniper berry, and rose hip.
- Medicinal **seeds** include milk thistle, chaste tree, fennel, and many members of the carrot family.
- Medicinal **roots** include Oregon grape, dandelion, burdock, and yellow dock.
- Medicinal **barks** include cramp bark, willow bark, and devil's club root bark.

There are some exceptions to this as some plants house their strongest medicine in multiple parts of their bodies. They will still have a peak time of potency.

When the terms **aerial parts** or **herb** are used, it refers to all aboveground parts of the plant being medicinal. These plants are usually harvested when in the flowering stage.

The term **whole plant** is used when the entire plant is considered medicinal. These plants have medicine throughout their whole bodies and are dug up, roots and all, when in the flowering stage.

We can now begin to see how each of the four seasons has a particular herbal focus because plants are in different stages of their growth cycles. We harvest the medicinal part of the plant at the time of year when the vital force is highest in that part of the plant's body. Energetically, the plant is sending more life force and vitality to a certain part of its body and not to others during its prime medicinal season. Herbally speaking, when a plant is sending its energy to a particular part, the majority of nutrients and medicinal constituents will be found there.

In spring when plants are sprouting up from the Earth, they are sending all their life energy to their brand-new baby green shoots and leaves. So spring is when we harvest the leaves—when they are fresh, vital, and loaded with nutrients.

When summer arrives and the plant has begun to flower, it is no longer the peak time to harvest the leaves, even though they may still be attached. The plants are now infusing their flowers with all their vitality in the hopes they'll be lucky enough to be pollinated. This is when we harvest flowers—when they are the most radiant and beautiful.

Come fall, the flowers have given way to the seed-bearing fruits, whose job it is to spread seed and ensure future generations. We harvest these fruits in fall—when their fruits look the most delectable.

Once winter arrives, the plant has already reproduced and spread seed. If it is a perennial, the energy and nutrients are sent underground as the plant hibernates, preparing to reemerge in spring. This is the optimal time to dig—when the life force and constituents are stored in the roots.

The general seasonal harvesting guidelines are:

* **Leaves** are harvested in spring.
* **Flowers** are harvested in summer.
* **Fruits** are harvested in late summer and early fall.
* **Seeds** are harvested in late summer and early fall.
* **Barks** are harvested in fall and spring.
* **Roots** are harvested in fall and winter.

It is important to note that this is a general rhythmic guideline and there are many exceptions. As much as we'd like it to, life does not fit into neat and tidy boxes that never deviate. Nature certainly doesn't behave this way and neither does the plant kingdom. Though there are exceptions to these guidelines, integrating the general what-and-why of this seasonal rhythm is enough to get our herbalism off and running, then the particulars of each individual plant are flushed out as we deepen our relationships with them.

Time

For first-time herb-workers, I recommend reading through all four seasonal chapters to incorporate an understanding of the energies and plants of the wheel of the year. Then, return to focus on the season you're currently in. For example, if it's summer, read through each season first and then return to summer. Once entering the current spot on the wheel of the year, read the opening spirit medicine of the season, do the seasonal meditation, and then grab your basket and get out there and look for those plants whose time is upon you. Meet, commune with, harvest, garble, make medicine from, and ingest the healing goodness of these ancient green ones. Their presence will facilitate the deeper reweaving while also filling your cabinets with healing medicines made from their very bodies.

A note about a seasonal approach and the modern calendar: The herbal wheel of the year shared here is not governed by the dominant modern Gregorian calendar as there is more fluctuation and nuance in nature than can be summarized by the modern approach to time-keeping. The approach of this book looks to the plants for orientation as to where we are on the wheel. Each location on Earth is different and each year is different in each location. Look to the plants to help find orientation. This capacity is in fact a deep hope for this book.

Here in the Olympic Mountains of the Pacific Northwest, the seasonal wheel of the year is often one to two months ahead of modern calendars. For example, by March 21, which is considered the "official" beginning of spring, the plants are usually well into their leafy growth. The nettle shoots and tree buds usually start popping out around mid-February. Looking to the plants for placement within the seasons helps us find our orientation as their bodies mirror the energies manifesting in our own bodies. Spring begins when the plants show us spring is beginning and when we feel spring occurring inside of our own bodies and spirits.

In the Pacific Northwest, by the "official" beginning of summer, June 21, the plants are well on their way to flowering. Summer solstice is the height, or peak, of summer's energies. Again looking to the plants for guidance, autumn here begins near the end of August, once the fruits and berries have set and are beginning to wither back. Winter sets in around mid-November, when most of the plant kingdom has died back, gone dormant, or retreated underground. Once the hard freeze of true winter hits, often the case by the "official" beginning of winter on December 21, the ground is too hard to dig roots from the Earth. There is usually a couple of months' break between the root harvest of winter and the first leafy harvest of spring.

Again, simply look to the plants to help find placement on the wheel of the year as our conscious awareness of the seasonal energies grows. After a few years of spiraling this way, we begin to simply feel the seasons within us as our own bodies, rewoven into the web of life, alert us to the seasonal changes.

Asking Permission

We always ask permission before plucking plants from the Earth. As our competency in plant communication deepens, the ability to be in conversation with the plants readily unfolds alongside it. It has been my experience that the ability to ask permission from the plants and receive, or perceive, the answer is an easily learned skill. Like all things, it develops with practice.

To ask permission to harvest a plant, first drop into the heart space, for it is in the heart that we communicate with our nonhuman kin. Once our heart is open, we can invite and tune into the energy of the plant. After that connection has been established, simply ask permission from the plant to harvest. Make sure the question feels authentic, humble, and honest, "May I harvest you?" The trick, especially for beginners, is to trust the heart to receive the answer as everyone experiences these subtle communications differently. Some people will hear a clear "yes" or "no" in their minds, while others will feel a certain set of body sensations that alert them to the answer. Personally, my heart opens and my body wants to lean in when the answer is "yes." When the answer is "no," my stomach closes down and my energy wants to pull in on itself. This relationship with my body cues has been developed over years of practice and is available to all who put in the time to practice.

Most, though not all the time, the plants say "yes" to our requests. If they say "no," the reason often reveals itself upon further communion and reflection. With further looking, we might realize that the location might not be the cleanest, perhaps having been recently sprayed or developed. Or we might realize that the plant stand wasn't quite big enough to sacrifice some of their population to harvest. Sometimes we don't know why the answer is "no." As good relatives, we obey the boundary and honor the "no," treating others the way we'd like to be treated.

Knowing the Area

When considering an area for wild harvesting, it helps to know the recent history of the land. We want to be certain that an area wasn't recently sprayed or developed and that we remain at least 100 feet away from any busy roads to avoid air pollutants. These measures all help avoid harvesting plants that have bioaccumulated toxins from the soil, water, or air. We also want to check on the harvesting laws of a given area. City, county, state, and national lands all have different laws regarding harvesting, some requiring special permits.

Over the years on the herbal walk, one ends up finding their own patches of plants—places they develop relationships with where the herbs that they utilize in their herbalism grow and willingly share of themselves.

Giving Thanks, Leaving Offerings

An exchange is always offered for the plants harvested by our hands. There are no specific rules for offerings, other than that the gift should come from the heart. Home crafting a blend of special offering herbs, especially those grown by our hands in our gardens, is a beautiful practice. This blend can be kept in a medicine pouch or bag that lives in our wildcrafting basket. After asking permission from a plant to harvest and receiving a "yes" in reply, we can leave a pinch of our offering blend on the ground, along with a prayer or statement of gratitude. If we forget our offering blend, or simply if we prefer, we can instead sing a song that we are guided to sing as our gift to the plant, leave a bite of our lunch, or offer a dance. What matters is that the gift authentically comes from our hearts, is accompanied by gratitude, and honors the sacrifice that the plants are making by allowing themselves to be harvested.

The importance of the heart-centered offering was driven home by my dear and generous herbal teacher, the hawthorn tree. I was harvesting hawthorn berries at a friend's home and had brought my young children with me for the occasion. Ordinarily, I take the time to say a prayer of heartfelt thanks when leaving an offering of tobacco before harvesting plants. This day, the kids were excited and all over the place and in the excitement I simply sprinkled the tobacco on the Earth without a prayer. The harvest, per usual with the generous hawthorn, was bountiful and abundant.

Upon returning home, I discovered I was missing one of the hand-beaded red earrings I had been wearing. I messaged my friend, asking her to keep an eye out for the earring. To neither of our surprise, she found it at the base of the hawthorn tree. That night, my friend, a powerful seer and dreamer, was given a dream. In the dream, she was sitting in front of the mother hawthorn and felt a knowing that when she had retrieved my earring, the balance of the offering had shifted. Hawthorn showed my sister dreamer that she, the hawthorn, liked the red beads of the earring because they matched the color of the berries she herself had offered us. Hawthorn showed that during the berry harvesting, we had accidentally broken one of her branches and so she felt that the broken earring was an equal exchange. My friend, still in the dream, asked hawthorn if we could bring different beads as well as honey, fresh cream, and bread in a clay bowl so that I could keep my very special earring. At this suggestion, the dream hawthorn shared a huge smile to communicate that she was content with that offering and, if implemented, the balance of exchange would be intact.

My friend felt a sense of urgency as though the replacement must happen the very next day. In the morning, she called me to share the dream and I too felt the urgency. I brought other red beads that were also very special to me and my heart and left them at the base of the hawthorn, along with a prayer of apology and authentic gratitude. My friend had already left out the bread, honey, and cream.

This powerful lesson, guided by the dreams and the spirit of hawthorn herself, drove home to me the importance and nuance of offerings and exchanges. The gift should come from the heart and be, or feel, equal in exchange for the sacrifice the plants are giving.

The "110 Percent Rule"

Compared to allopathic medicines like pharmaceuticals and over-the-counter drugs, herbs are wildly safe with exponentially fewer side effects and fewer interactions with drugs. That being said, it is still imperative to have a strong orientation toward safety woven into our herbal explorations.

When it comes to our wild harvesting, a rule we can remember and implement is what I like to call the "110 Percent Rule." The rule goes like this: We must be 110 percent certain of the exact identity of a plant we are considering harvesting and ingesting. The 110 percent, which my husband likes to point out is not mathematically possible or correct, sticks in our minds, reminding us to triple-check our presumptions and make sure there is not even a microscopic sliver of doubt. We want to know, with full-body certainty in every cell of our being, the correct identity of the plant we are harvesting.

Remember, herbalism is a wisdom walk and wisdom requires humility. When we aren't certain, when we feel the slightest whisper of doubt or tickle of concern, we should listen to that wisdom voice and wait to gather more information before proceeding. When we are less than 110 percent certain, it's a great time to reconsult our plant field guide or snap a picture and send it to an herbal friend. There are even fancier support methods these days, with smartphone plant identification apps readily available.

Harvesting with Future Generations in Mind

No more than 10 percent of a given plant stand should be removed by our hands. We don't want to come even close to harvesting so much that it will impact a plant's ability to maintain its population and ensure its continued survival. The grandmothers and grandfathers of a patch ought to be left alone out of respect for the elders and in honor of their much-deserved place of exaltation. All efforts are made to leave no trace of our harvest, with no gaping holes or upturned land left in our wake.

Most herbal harvesting endeavors can be accomplished with a small number of tools that comprise our wild harvesting kit or basket.

* **A basket, bucket, or bags** to hold the harvest. Gently used baskets are often readily available at secondhand stores.
* **Offering blends** can be carried in a medicine bag hung around the neck, a fanny pack around the waist, or tucked into a harvest basket.
* **Garden shears** for cutting stems, small branches, and thicker leaves.
* **Snips** for working with daintier and less fibrous plant parts like leaves and flowers.
* **Loppers** for trimming or removing branches and other more fibrous or woody plant parts.

- **A hori hori,** part blade and part shovel, for help digging smaller roots like dandelion and Oregon grape.

- **A digging fork** for digging up deeper roots like burdock and comfrey.

- **A utility knife** for times when a sharp blade is needed.

- **Plant field guides.** For those residing in the Pacific Northwest, the two books *Plants of the Pacific Northwest Coast* by Jim Pojar and Andy MacKinnon and *Pacific Northwest Medicinal Plants* by Scott Kloos will become old friends and trusted allies.[1,2] For non-Pacific Northwesterners, seek out a local plant field guide to help with identification. Most regions in North America have fabulous plant guides available.

Garbling

After our harvest has been made, it is time to turn the bodies of these plants into medicine for the people. "Garbling" is the delightfully old-timey word herbalists use to describe the act of processing plants into their most optimal and potent medicinal form, encompassing how we prepare plants' bodies into medicine for the people. Garbling is the essential step before medicine-making, which we explore in detail in later chapters. To help get the idea, here are a handful of garbling examples.

- To garble hawthorn leaf and flower, pluck the medicinal flowers and leaves from the stems, discarding the stems.

* To garble nettle leaves, remove any browned, moldy, or decaying leaves and discard them.

* To garble chickweed, sift through the pile of plant material, removing any twigs, sticks, grass, etc., that might have gotten mixed in with the chickweed.

* To garble rose petals, pluck the petals from the flower heads and discard all but the fragrant petals.

* To garble rose hips, slice open the hips to scrape out and discard the inner hairs and seeds, leaving only the juicy medicinal flesh.

* To garble devil's club, scrape off the outer bark to reveal the inner bark, then whittle the inner bark from the woody core.

Monographs

A practice many herbal learners find useful is the habit of documenting all they are learning about medicinal plants. These *monographs* contain detailed information on a plant's many attributes and are the place to capture all that is learned and experienced throughout our herbal journey and studies. Here is a sample template I've used in my journal.

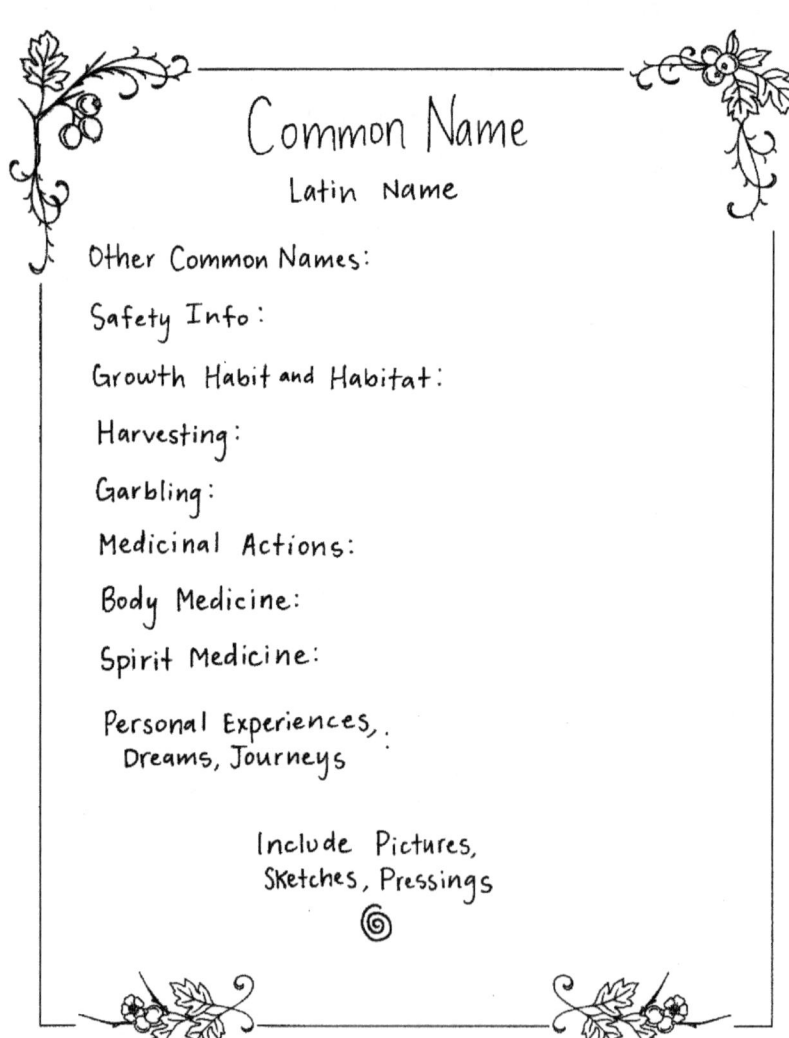

A Note on Accessibility

One doesn't need to live in the wild, near the wild, or have access to the wild to practice the herbalism that follows. Nor are living close to nature or having space to garden requirements to be considered an "herbalist." I lived in a tiny basement apartment in Seattle for the majority of my time as an herbalist. My encounters with the plants in the pages that follow happened during walks on city streets and forays into city parks, with the occasional opportunity to head into the wild. Most of the plants in this section can be easily found growing in cities, parks, and abandoned or disturbed spaces. Herbalism can be practiced anywhere if we just know where to look, what to look for, and, most importantly, how to orient our minds and hearts to the search.

The Herbal Wheel of the Year

There are nineteen plants for us to get to know this year. Rose shows up in two seasons because her body gives us powerful medicine twice a year. Most of these plants are found growing wild across North America. Two that are unique to the West Coast, red cedar and devil's club, could be added to the landscape with a bit of know-how. Raspberry, calendula, and comfrey are not native to North America, though they are well on their way to being fully naturalized and integrated into many landscapes and can likely be found growing near where the people grow.

Each plant has a synopsis of healing attributes that are helpful and utilized in basic folk herbalism. Remember that plants are dynamic creatures. Their medicine is complex and multifaceted. The medicinal descriptions are intentionally on the shorter side to make the plants, and herbalism, feel and be more approachable to the beginner.

Spiritual gifts of the plants are shared as received from communion time with the plants and teachings I've received in dreams. Plants are vastly complex beings, constantly unveiling deeper layers of themselves as the years go by and the relationships deepen. My plant-spirit medicine interactions are shared in hopes of opening the door and inspiring your own to blossom.

In the **Preparations** section, suggested herbal remedies are shared that have proven helpful and versatile in the practice of home folk herbalism. In later chapters, we traverse the magical terrain of medicine-making, with detailed how-tos on whipping up medicinal preparations from these beloved plants.

Note: If you encounter a term you are unfamiliar with, such as "acetract," "liniment," or "tincture," take a peek at Part 3 of the book for more details on herbal preparations. The Glossary (page 273) and Index (page 285) are great resources for new-to-you terms found throughout the herbal wheel of the year.

Each plant includes one **Herbal Formula.** Wherever possible, the formulas include other plants that appear in this book, along with widely available plants found in North America.

Each season ends with a **Going Deeper** section. This is for folks who might have a bit more herbal experience under their belts or are simply on fire in love with herbalism right now and want to dive in as deep as possible. Additional plants are listed who are medicinal and prime for harvest each season. Simply apply the same seasonal herbalism principles to encounters with these other plants to expand the herbal repertoire. Enjoy the journey!

PART 2:
The Herbal Wheel of the Year

"For if we can learn to intuitively sense the changes in the natural renewing energies of the seasons and begin to live in alignment with the sacred movements of the Earth . . . the power of these seasonal events will breathe new life into us in profound and powerful ways. We are in a time when people the world over have spiritually devolved and lost connection with their seasonal and celestial senses. The good news is that it's not difficult to rebuild our relationship with the Earth . . . The memories of these ways are literally part of our ancestral blood memory . . . We may have forgotten the words of our original song, but we can hum along until we begin to remember again."

— *Doug Good Feather, Lakota leader and author of* <u>Think Indigenous</u>[1]

Chapter 4: Spring

Spring Spirit Walk

Come join me on a walk through the wild on this early spring day.

The first thing we notice is the return of the birdsong. After a long winter of darkness, stillness, and silence, here they are, our winged kin, having returned from their winter migrations. We thank the birds for reminding us that our song always returns through every turn of the cycle. We feel the stir of our own soul-songs begin to run through our veins.

Many deciduous trees greet us this morning. Gazing at these standing ones, we feel the slightest invigoration, a zing, a spark coursing through our blood. In our hearts, we feel the trees simply chuckle and say, "Your sap is rising too, eh little ones," their bodies reflecting the emergent spring energies that are arising within our own.

We take a deep breath, chuckling back with them and adding in a sigh that almost sounds like a song. We feel hopeful, invigorated, a burst of energy within. We keep walking and as we do, we look down to the skin of Mother Earth where we see . . . Could it be? The baby nettles are poking through! "You are here!" we say with excitement. "We almost doubted you would return."

"Oh young ones," we feel their giggle in our hearts. "Rebirth always happens. We always come back. This is the way of things. And so it is for you too."

Tears are brought to our eyes as our faith in the ever-turning wheel of the year washes over our hearts, cleansing any doubts that spring might not have come. Our hearts open to remember we belong here, to this place, this Earth, this web of life. We, like these plants, are spring-ing! Our burdens, doubts, and fears are washed away in the mirroring presence of these ancient baby green ones re-membering us into being.

"Thank you," we say through tears, prostrating ourselves to be at their level and bowing to their short little magnificence.

"Always, little ones," our hearts hear them respond. "And don't forget to come back and pick us later. Your bodies need to be washed out just as your hearts and spirits were a moment ago by those tears! We would like to help you with that."

Our gratitude for the noble nettles overflows the cup in our hearts as we say, "How can we give back to you?"

"Sing your songs out into the world. And as your songs sing, they will join in harmony with the other soul-songs. And the people will re-member."

So we sing them a song now, a song that arises spontaneously from our hearts and it is the song of the plants, of spring, of this moment. We walk on, resolved to shed whatever winter heaviness we've been carrying and sing our soul-songs out into this world. We do so in gratitude to the plants for their constant reminders and reflections of our belonging to this web of life.

We pause and chuckle after this interaction, remembering this same time, these same energies, this same spark, same zing, same spirit we felt last year at this time. Oh yes, spring is here.

Later we return to this spot with our offering bags, snips, and harvest basket to take home the bodies of these nettles that offered themselves to us. We give a nice pinch from our offering bag and say a gratitude blessing for all of life to be served by the nettles' sacrifice. Spring is here and that means that the busy herbal harvest season is beginning!

Spring Spirit Medicine
Spring rebirths us. The season of spring calls us awake and alive from our long winter gestation and hibernation. During spring, our vibrancy returns. Our light and energy are reawakening. Our spirits are being reborn.

Spring is hope. The promise of spring is the promise of hope. When spring returns, hope incarnates into all of nature, guaranteeing us that life is indeed continuing. A great relief and gratitude rinse through us as we receive this great mercy that is life continued.

Spring invigorates us. The return of life, growth, and actualized hope invigorate the soul and a strong holy impulse to live again, to live well, and to work and serve on behalf of all of life courses through our veins.

Spring Spirit Medicine Reflections

On a day when spring energies are high, find a spot in nature where your eyes are drawn into the presence of new life emerging from the plant world. Perhaps there are tiny sprouts or the leaves of bulbs popping up from the ground. Or perhaps the eyes land upon swelling buds on the shrubs and deciduous trees. Breathe in the energy of this place, this time, this feeling. This is the spirit medicine of spring, that which is stirring inside of you. In this place, reflect on the following questions.

* What new life is growing or wants to be growing within me this year?
* What dreams or creations are growing within me?
* What am I letting go of in order that these new sprouts might grow?
* What roots am I setting down in order to weave myself even more deeply into relationship with the web of life?
* How might these new growths within me serve all of Creation?
* How can I give back to feed all of life?

Spring Herbalism

In early springtime, perennial plants, or those whose bodies live more than one year, are waking up from the sleep within their underground roots or dormant buds and are sprouting back toward the light of the Sun. Annual plants, those whose bodies live only one year, are seeds sprouting into the dawn of the beginning of their lives.

Spring is the time of medicinal leaves. During spring, we see the new green shoots, buds, and leaves from the plants. Because the plants are not yet focused on growing tall or setting their flowers or fruits, all their energy and vitality is being sent into those little leaves, leaflets, and shoots. These little green growing plant bodies are loaded with the perfect cocktails of chemicals and nutrients to grow the plants' bodies strong in the growing season to come.

Spring plants are cleansing. The chemicals and nutrients in those bursting little plant shoots, leaves, and buds are major cleansing medicine for the bodies of the people. Generally, spring leaves are detoxifying, blood-cleansing, nutritive, and revitalizing. They support our organs of detoxification with the shaking off of the stagnation of winter.

Spring plants are bitter. These leaves, shoots, and sprouts often have one thing in common: They are bitter! And that bitter flavor is a large part of the medicine our human bodies need to snap us awake and kick on our internal detoxification mechanisms. Bitter plants stimulate the secretion of our digestive juices and stimulate our liver, gallbladder, and bowels. Simply grazing on the leaflets and buds bursting forth from nature during early spring provides a powerful cleansing for our human bodies. Remember the 110 Percent Rule and then graze away.

NETTLE
Urtica dioica

Body Parts: Leaves and baby shoots before they reach two feet tall—the smaller the better

Other Parts at Other Times:
- Late Summer — Snip off seed heads.
- Fall/Winter — Dig up rhizomes.

Harvesting: Nettle stings, so wear gloves. There is a way to harvest the nettles barehanded that minimizes stinging, but this requires going slow with a deep and intimate knowledge of the plant's body. After many years of deep relationship with nettle, I personally still wear gloves about half the time.

Safety: Do not harvest after the plant reaches around two feet in height as they can form compounds that are hard on the kidneys. After being cooked or dried, nettle loses its sting.

Nettle is new life. One of my fondest memories is when my daughter was only six weeks old. It was our first spring living amidst the wild forest that is now our home and it was the spring season in the spring chapter of my life. Hope, growth, and vitality permeated my atmospheres. I was hired to harvest thirteen pounds of fresh nettle shoots for a local herbal tincture company. As I was still freshly postpartum and in recovery after a difficult birth, my physical health was subpar. So I recruited my husband to help with the job. Of course my newborn daughter joined. The three of us spent an entire afternoon, snip-snip-snipping, nettle shoot by nettle shoot. My daughter lay on her back on a blanket, staring at the play of lights on the budding trees and the light of Father Sky. I would take breaks to breastfeed her whenever she needed. It was hard work. Thirteen pounds of any herb is a lot! But our little family completed the task and that nettle harvest helped template a life of herbal abundance, stewardship, caretaking, and cycling with the plants that has set the tone for us since.

Herbalist and master wildcrafter Scott Kloos says of nettle, "As one of the first harvests of the year, I encourage using this experience [of harvesting nettle] as an opportunity to affirm careful and attentive harvesting practices in preparation for the wildcrafting season that will follow."[1] Nettle really does kick off the growing times, calling our inner wildcrafters back to life from their winter gestations and rests.

Nettle stings. The sting in nettle is due to a whole cocktail of inflammatory substances living in the very tips of the hairs on the leaves and stems of the plant. The cocktail includes, among other things, histamine and formic acid. Thankfully, the constituents in the stinging cocktail are extremely unstable and will dissipate when the plant is dried, cooked, blended, pureed, or juiced. There is nothing dangerous about the sting. Usually any skin irritation will heal rather quickly, though some folks are much more sensitive to the sting and can find it very uncomfortable. Folks who are not as sensitive might allow themselves to be intentionally stung throughout the season to receive the blood cleansing, anti-inflammatory, and immune-flushing benefits it provides. In the past, this process was called "urtication" and referred to the therapeutic flogging of nettles for immune-enhancing benefits.

Nettle nourishes. Nettle is deeply nutritive and can and should be consumed as food. Substitute nettle for any cooked leafy green in a recipe. Nettle is a powerhouse of minerals and vitamins, containing silica, calcium, iron, potassium, vitamin A, vitamin D, and vitamin C. Nettle builds the health of blood, bone, hair, skin, and nails. Nettle nourishes the adrenal glands, promoting feelings of mental clarity, vitality, and overall well-being.

Nettle revitalizes. Nettle is one of those plants that we can really *feel* when we ingest. Nettle increases the feelings of vitality, vigor, and good green life energy coursing through the veins. By restoring the adrenals, nettle is very revitalizing and can be consumed by anyone who wants to increase their energy levels.

Nettle clears out the old. Nettle decreases inflammation, supports the kidneys, lymph, and liver in detoxification, and alkalizes the body. Think of nettle anytime the body needs some extra detoxification support, especially if there is pain, swelling, or skin inflammation manifesting due to a lack of proper detoxification. Nettle will help without harming.

Nettle helps us embody. Nettle is pure nourishment and grounding, connecting us to the core of our nature and vitality. Anytime we are feeling ungrounded or disconnected, nettle can remind us what it means to have bodies on this Earth that need to be tended to and nourished. Loaded with minerals, nettle connects us to the Earth of our beings.

Nettle enlivens. Nettle is zesty, fiery, and stimulating. The sting teaches us that fire and zest are important and essential to life. The fact that the pain of the sting is also healing to deeper pains in the body alerts us of the necessity to "light a fire" sometimes to get life energy moving and flowing. Nettle stimulates our spirit fires and passion for life. Consider sitting with nettle when the passion and zest for life might be diminished, whether it is the physical life force needing nourishment or the spirit life force needing spark and inspiration.

Nettle holds the wisdom of an elder crone. Nettle's spirit holds the vibration of an elder crone, the wise woman archetype. She is the old woman who has lived a full life, faced many trials and tribulations, seen it all, and assimilated all of that life experience into wisdom. Wisdom shines through her eyes and the spark of life has not gone out in her. She is still living a full fiery life. She knows who she is and what she knows. She also knows how to tell it like it is. Connect with nettle in times when we need a good taste of elder medicine, an encounter with true and real wisdom, and when we need to get "whipped into shape" by hearing potentially hard truths.

Nettle teaches boundaries. Another medicine of the wise woman crone that nettle teaches us to emulate is the ability to swiftly and fiercely set a boundary (a sting!) to get us youngsters in line. What exactly are the boundaries that nettle is enforcing? The boundaries of wisdom, alignment with the forces of life, and the very laws of nature herself. Perhaps we're moving too fast, not being thoughtful enough, not paying proper respects, inadvertently violating others' boundaries, unintentionally violating the laws of reciprocity, and the like. In these instances, in no subtle way, nettle teaches us about the righteous and proper implementation of boundaries in our lives. Nettle is a powerful teacher to sit with when we are working to integrate stronger boundaries. Generally, nettle will show us the way.

Harvest huge amounts — Just for personal use, I will cover a king-size bed sheet to dry out and store in garbage bags for the year. The more, the better.

Eat fresh or freeze fresh — Blanch and freeze the nettles in quart-size bags for tossing into stir-fries, soups, stews, fresh pestos, etc.

Dry for infusions — We can't drink too much nettle tea. Steep ½ to 1 cup of the dried leaves overnight in a quart of water, then drink the next day. This way of making teas is a major mineral elixir.

Dry for smoothies — There's no reason for those of us who grow where nettle grows to ship in any other chlorophyll- and mineral-rich greens for our smoothie additions. We have nettle! In smoothies, 1 to 2 dried tablespoons is a fabulous nourishing and alkalizing greens powder.

Acetract — Infuse nettles in balsamic vinegar, apple cider vinegar, or both to use in cooking, dressings, and drizzles throughout the year. An apple cider vinegar nettle acetract is a fabulous hair rinse tonic.

Tincture — So much of nettle's medicine comes from its high mineral content and minerals are generally not well extracted in alcohol. So even though nettle is stronger as tea, vinegar, or food, keep the tincture on hand for detox formulas, anti-inflammatory support, and to engage with for spirit medicine.

Herbal Formula: Spring Cleanse Tea

This delicious tea is blood-cleansing and nourishing. It is excellent to take as a gentle spring cleanse to call us out of the hibernating and stagnating time of winter. The herbs help to cleanse and cool our blood, providing a gentle but powerful detox. It's a great cleanse to do if we are prone to allergies or skin challenges at the turn to spring.

Combine the following dried herbs.

1 ounce nettle leaf
½ ounce cleavers leaf and stem
½ ounce horsetail herb
½ ounce red clover herb
½ ounce peppermint or lemon balm herb

Steep 4 tablespoons of the tea blend in 1 quart of water each morning. Steep for 15 minutes, then strain and drink throughout the day. Repeat each day for 1 to 2 weeks.

Other Formulas:
Womb Love Tea page 101

CHICKWEED
Stellaria media

Body Parts: Aerial parts

Harvesting: Chickweed is most certainly growing somewhere close by as this delightful and dainty plant loves to grow close to where people grow. Chickweed can be found peppering lawns, yards, woodland environments, disturbed areas, and the like and is very easy to harvest. Take scissors and snip just above the ground in a patch of chickweed, almost "hand-mowing" the patch to harvest the aerial parts, stems, flowers, leaves, and all. Because it grows in lawn-like environments, it's a good idea to sift through after harvesting to make certain other plants, such as grasses and other "weeds," didn't sneak in during the hand-mowing.

Chickweed clears. Chickweed is a powerful cleansing spring tonic with a strong lymphagogue property. Lymphagogues support the lymphatic system in its important detoxification work by promoting circulation and the removal of toxins throughout the body. When there is lymphatic stagnation, chickweed clears. It also helps support and cleanse the kidneys and supports healthy, radiant skin.

Chickweed nourishes. Chickweed is a healing food, delicious to graze on and add to our salads, smoothies, sandwiches, and snacks. The herb is loaded with good absorbable nutrients, such as B vitamins, the minerals magnesium, iron, potassium, zinc, and selenium, and even the bioflavonoid quercetin.

Chickweed cools. Chickweed is an old folk remedy for weight loss and cellulite when taken internally, believed to help the body break down toxic metabolites that cause weight retention. Chickweed helps to cool the body and blood when there is excess heat. Call upon chickweed for hot flashes and night sweats, red skin and rosacea, and a general inflamed, red-hot state as chickweed will cool down the situation.

Chickweed helps the itchies. Chickweed is a topical anti-itch herb par excellence. In Europe, popular chickweed creams are made and sold to help take down the inflammation from dermatitis, eczema, psoriasis, and other red-hot inflammatory skin conditions. Chickweed is a most excellent herb to include in salves for topical skin care and healing, essential to have around for first aid skin situations like bug bites, bee stings, rashes, and the like.

Chickweed is stellar. The Latin name *Stellaria* alerts us to chickweed's stellar nature. Look closely at chickweed's little white flowers and you will notice that they are little stars! The "little star lady," as herbal teacher Susun Weed calls her,[2] cools and enlightens, showing us that we can let go of old stories, release energetic stagnation, and undo tethers to the past. We can forgive, open the heart, and move on. Chickweed helps us in the clearing of bitterness and resentment, old grievances, old stories, and old baggage. Chickweed reflects to us the starry nature of our beings and the ability to always choose new light. Chickweed lightens and uplifts the spirit, restoring the magic of our child-like nature and wonder.

Chickweed is ancient. Chickweed connects us to the stream of Grandmother Wisdom and simple folk medicine, that ancient lineage from all times and everywhere of women who knew how to access the plants and the mysteries of the Earth to keep the people well. "The lovely lowly chickweed with its cool blue jewels is a feminine herb that could not survive the masculine phase of decadent Galenic medicine," says herbalist Peter Holmes so perfectly to explain how on Earth this powerhouse of a medicinal herb could have fallen out of popular use.[3] Chickweed teaches us that we can "stay close to the Earth to avoid the gaze of evil" and continue on nourishing, nurturing, and feeding life. Chickweed teaches us that the best medicine is growing right outside our doors, is in season, and is best when eaten fresh. Chickweed reweaves us into closer connection with the parts of our own lineages that walked in this way of rewoven Earth herbalism.

Eat fresh — Chickweed really is best and most powerful when eaten fresh. Top priority should be finding patches of chickweed around the home to graze upon. Add to salads, sandwiches, smoothies, and soups, and munch on it plain.

Tincture fresh — Chickweed tincture is great to have around to add to joint and skin cleansing formulas and general detoxification support.

Freeze — Puree chickweed with a bit of water and freeze fresh in ice cube trays. These little frozen gems are great to have when there's a bug bite, bee sting, itchy skin, rash, hives, etc. They are so very cooling to the skin and help to take the itch away.

Infused oil — Chickweed is absolutely an herb to infuse in oil and have on hand to whip into an all-purpose skin-healing salve. Chickweed helps to decrease the itching from bites and stings and to cool and heal inflammatory skin conditions.

Herbal Formula: Skin-Healer Salve

This is an all-purpose skin salve to apply to all manner of skin situations, including itchies, bites, scrapes, cuts, infections, rashes, burns, dry skin, etc.

Prepare an oil infusion of equal parts of the following plants.

Chickweed aerial parts
St. John's wort leaf and flower
Calendula flower
Self-heal aerial parts
Plantain leaf

Add beeswax to turn the oil into a salve. To each cup of herbal salve you prepare, add 20 drops of lavender essential oil.

Other Formulas:
Healthy Skin Drops page 198

CLEAVERS
Galium aparine

Body Parts: Leaves and stems

Harvesting: Cleavers is very easy to harvest and can likely be found growing in the neighborhood in or around garden beds and lawns. It will make itself known by sticking to our clothes. Considered a pesky weed by many, most people are thrilled and surprised to discover that this weed they often pull out is a medicinal plant. You will know cleavers by its sticky nature. Very easy to harvest, simply pull clumps of the sticky herb out of the ground and process from there.

Cleavers cleanses. Cleavers is a powerful cleansing spring tonic that helps pull us out of winter stagnation, renewing and revitalizing our bodies and spirits. Like all of the spring tonics, cleavers supports the body generally in its detoxification work, cooling and cleansing the entire system. Cleavers has a special affinity for and association with the waters of the body, supporting the urinary and lymphatic systems.

Cleavers loves the lymph. Cleavers is a powerful lymphagogue, helping promote circulation through the lymphatic system, relieving lymphatic congestion and water retention. Think of cleavers when there is swelling, stagnation, or swollen lymph glands. Cleavers will gently and effectively help get the lymph moving.

Cleavers clears the ears. Cleavers helps generally with lymphatic swelling and congestion anywhere in the body, though it has a special affinity for the inner ear, sinus, and throat areas. In the case of ear infection, whether single or recurring, cleavers helps to clear the congestion and excess fluid associated with infection. It also helps clear up lingering sinus congestion and aid recovery from sinus infection.

Cleavers clears the skin. Because of its lymph and blood-cleansing effects, cleavers is a wonderful support for clearing up the underlying causes leading to skin challenges. In the case of acne, eczema, dermatitis, psoriasis, and other inflammatory skin situations, cleavers will help the body rid itself of toxins so they do not need to be expressed through the skin.

Cleavers is playful. The spirit of cleavers is joyful, playful, silly, and heart-opening. "Cleavers cling to cleavage," I say to students when teaching about this herb's sticky nature, always to much laughter. Children of all ages love cleavers and simply gazing upon the unique sticky psychedelic body of this plant effortlessly opens and lightens the heart. Cleavers teaches us to not take our lives too seriously, nurture the divine child within, and lighten up to the forces of life.

Cleavers restores flow. Cleavers are very watery plants. Their bodies are wet and juicy and they have a special affinity for the waters of our bodies. Cleavers can help us when the watery natures of our spirits are stuck, if we are having a hard time letting go, or feel weighed down by boggy emotions. Cleavers helps restore us to the flow of life, the great gift of water. Cleavers provides gentle soul-cleansing, clearing the spirit of old stickiness that helps us reconnect to joy, childlike innocence, and curiosity. When life seems to have taken these away due to sorrow and hardship, cleavers helps to restore hope and usher in the new.

Cleavers cleave. Cleavers helps us to cut ties and "cleave" off that which is no longer serving us. The sticky nature of cleavers helps us to let go of even the hard sticky stuff and cleavers is fabulous in helping us let go of old patterns and unhealthy relationships that we just seem to be stuck in. Cleavers helps cut these tethers from our sticky pasts and washes us anew.

Dry for infusion — Cleavers deserves a spot in most detoxifying tea blends, whether for skin support, joint inflammation, lymph clearing, or seasonal cleansing.

Tincture — The tincture is wonderful for the reasons above and to add to formulas for decongesting the ears and sinuses.

Herbal Formula: Love Your Lymph Tincture

This is a gentle yet powerful blend of local wild lymphagogue and alterative herbs. We might take this tincture for a spring cleanse, when we're feeling a little lymphy or swollen, or when struggling with skin issues.

Prepare a tincture of fresh or dried herbs using the following proportions.

30% cleavers leaf and stem
25% burdock root
25% dandelion root
20% red clover flower

Directions: Consider taking 1 to 2 droppersful 3x daily when on a lymph-clearing program.

Other Formulas:
Spring Cleanse Tea page 82
Healthy Skin Drops page 198

MUGWORT
Artemisia spp.

Note: The genus *Artemisia* contains numerous medicinal plants, most of whom are strong-acting in both their physical and spiritual medicines. In some cases, they are quite different from one another. Identify the *Artemisia* species that grow locally in your bioregion. Here in the Pacific Northwest, we have *Artemisia suksdorfii,* also known as coastal mugwort, and *Artemisia ludoviciana,* also known as western mugwort. The European mugwort *Artemisia vulgaris* can be found growing wild as a garden escapee and in the past was even included on Washington state's noxious weed list.

Body Parts: Leaves

Other Parts at Other Times:
- Summer — The flowers and stalks are also medicinal.

Harvesting: The stalks of mugwort are also considered medicinal, so the harvest is typically some combination of leaves and stalks. Use snips or scissors to trim the daintier stalks and leaves, discarding the more fibrous central stalks.

Safety: Mugwort is not appropriate to ingest when trying to conceive, pregnant, or breastfeeding.

Mugwort invigorates the womb. One of mugwort's best-known indications is as a remedy to clear the womb. The herb, being sacred to the Moon, has a powerful link to the uterus and its ability to increase circulation to the womb space is not to be underestimated. Mugwort can be utilized when there's pelvic stagnation or congestion that is causing uncomfortable PMS symptoms, menstrual cramping, and delayed menses, or unwanted pregnancies. The magnetic Moon-pull of mugwort will pull new blood and life force into the womb and stimulate the uterus's ability to cleanse itself. This works when the plant is ingested internally and when applied topically as an infused oil.

Mugwort promotes circulation. When applied topically as an infused oil, mugwort acts powerfully to promote circulation to otherwise underfed areas of the body. The plant is helpful for sore muscles, aches, bruises, and areas with less than optimal circulation.

Mugwort is diaphoretic. Mugwort helps support the body through colds, flus, and other feverish states by reliably promoting sweating and helping to break fevers. The antimicrobial, bronchodilating, and warming effects of the plant generally make it a helpful ally for fevers and flus.

Mugwort is bitter. A little goes a long way. The bitter principle in mugwort is strong. The plant has a generally stimulating, clearing, and tonifying effect on the digestive tract. When a few drops of tincture are taken before meals, it can help to improve digestive function and power, thereby decreasing after-meal gas and bloating. It has this same effect when taken before bedtime, in addition to promoting dreams as described below. The *Artemisias* in general have a strong antiparasitic and antifungal effect and are often utilized to help correct digestive imbalances of this nature.

Mugwort weaves dreams. In old European folklore, mugwort is known for its dreamweaving qualities. The plant is sacred to the Moon, the celestial body often cited as the bringer and mirror of the people's dreams. Mugwort is food for the dreaming spirit within us all. Engaging with mugwort in a conscious way before entering sleep—either by drinking tea, burning smudge, anointing with an infused oil, or all of these—reliably softens the dream door, granting us deeper access to the dreaming realms and improving our likelihood of "catching the dreams" upon awakening. I have observed hundreds of students in my dreaming classes over the years reclaim and grow their inner dreamer by working with mugwort as a plant guardian and dream teacher. This is a great blessing indeed as once the dreaming is reclaimed, life takes on a more numinous, more purposeful, and, dare I say, more *magical* tonal quality.

Mugwort is euphoric. How does mugwort accomplish this dreamweaving? Believe it or not, the medicine is a purely spiritual one, for there are no entheogenic, psychoactive, or hallucinogenic compounds to be found in the plant. In other words, mugwort is not forcing open the psychic veil or significantly shifting brain neurochemistry. Her action is subtle yet powerful. She brings the dreams naturally, though undeniably. This effect can be called "euphoric." The spirit of mugwort helps to shift the consciousness and energy into a state of euphoria, or drowsy subtle pleasure—the state that makes us more receptive to our dream source. Mugwort moves our rational waking egos out of the way so that we can soften into the natural state and spiritual function that is dreaming and being dreamt.

Mugwort empowers the wild feminine. The name *Artemisia* was given to these plants in honor of the Greek goddess Artemis, a virgin huntress of the Wild Hunt, of the Moon, and of herbalism. Artemis is and represents the spirit force of the feminine who is fierce, sovereign unto herself, answers to no one, and is fully embodying and incarnating her wild feminine power—a revolutionary act in a patriarchal epoch. Mugwort helps awaken this aspect of feminine power, sovereignty, and wild strength. Artemis is a patron goddess of midwives. Indeed mugwort helps to keep the womb chi flowing strongly and clearly, including bringing on a moonflow if a woman so chooses.

Dry for infusion — A little goes a long way with mugwort as the plant is quite bitter. Just a pinch will do for crafting a nighttime dream tea. The dried leaves also lend themselves beautifully to bath blends that promote sleeping and dreaming.

Tincture — The tincture is strong and bitter, not one to be taken in high doses at regular intervals. However, adding smaller amounts to tincture blends for reproductive and immune health is common.

Infused oil — A lovely green infused oil can be made from mugwort leaves that serves many purposes. It can be applied as an anointing oil for the dreams before bed, as a tonic for the reproductive system or feminine spirit when applied over the womb, or generally as a muscle support and circulatory promoter for the whole body.

Herbal Formula: Dreamweaver Tea

This blend of mugwort and relaxing nervine herbs helps to guide and nudge the body toward sleep in a gentle manner while nudging open the dream door so that we can have greater access to this source of wisdom.

Prepare a tea blend of dried herbs using the following proportions.

30% chamomile flower
20% mugwort leaf
20% lemon balm herb
20% oatseed
10% lavender flower

Drink 1 cup at night before bed to promote sleeping and dreaming.

Other Formulas:
Womb Love Tea page 101

RASPBERRY
Rubus ideaus

Body Parts: Leaves

Harvesting: Use scissors or snips to harvest these delicate green leaves.

Safety: Though raspberry leaf has a long folk legacy of ingestion during pregnancy, recent concerns have arisen that question its safety. Pregnant women should check with their own medical support team and inner guidance to decide for themselves. My two cents is to avoid raspberry leaf (and most things, really) in the first trimester of pregnancy and to take it under medical supervision in the second and third trimesters.

Raspberry loves the womb. Raspberry leaves are powerful. nourishing, and tonifying medicine for the uterus, helping to empower and optimize uterine function. They are rich in minerals and other constituents that nourish, feed, and tone the uterus. Though most widely known for pregnancy support, raspberry leaves are nutritious and tonifying in all cycles of life. Raspberry leaves' effect on the uterus is balancing, they have a true amphoteric effect, helping restore this sacred space to optimal homeostatic function regardless of the direction of imbalance. Raspberry leaves are an excellent reproductive and fertility tonic, overall improving the vigor and tone of the uterus and improving its ability to receive, grow, and deliver new life. As a pelvic decongestant, raspberry leaves help increase the flow of blood, lymph, and life force through the entire pelvis. This can bring healing energy and potential relief into the pelvis for all kinds of pelvic challenges, including PMS, menstrual cramps, fibroids, low libido, amenorrhea, pelvic discomfort, and more.

Raspberry nurtures the feminine. Raspberry is a beautiful, powerful medicine to teach us about grounded feminine empowerment, embodying many aspects of the beautiful and sacred feminine nature.

Raspberry is nourishing. The berries are incredibly nourishing and so are the leaves. The leaves are loaded with minerals that build uterine endurance. Raspberry leaves are softening. Just touching the body of the dried leaves softens the spirit. They teach us how we can be soft and strong at the same time as we nurture life. Raspberry softens the edges of tough initiations (childbirth, anyone?) while connecting us to the ancient lineage of grandmothers and ancestors. Raspberry very much holds the frequency of "women's mysteries" and teaches us about the power of the feminine spirit. Work with raspberry medicine when undergoing any menstrual mystery initiation to help soften into surrender.

Dry for infusions — Tea is the optimal form for raspberry as the leaves are so loaded with minerals. Minerals extract better in water. The tea is also delicious! Sweet, soft, and a bit bitter, raspberry leaves make a lovely hot or cold nourishing tea. They also mix very well with others.

Tincture fresh — The tincture is a worthy addition to the home tincture apothecary. It can be added to formulas as a pelvic decongestant and overall restorer of womb and pelvic health.

Herbal Formula: Womb Love Tea

This tea promotes circulation and chi flow to the womb and provides nourishment, grounding, cleansing, and invigoration. Drink this tea in all kinds of challenges or wellnesses and stages of life when the womb space could use some extra lovin'.

Prepare a tea blend of dried herbs using the following amounts.

1 ounce raspberry leaf
½ ounce mugwort leaf
½ ounce nettle leaf
½ ounce red clover flower
½ ounce wild rose petal
¼ ounce ginger root

Prepare a quart of tea in the morning at a dose of 4 tablespoons per quart of water. Steep for 30 minutes, strain, and sip throughout the day.

Going Deeper into Spring

In the Wild

Plantain leaf — Plantain grows everywhere. Learning to identify plantain grants a steady supply of vulnerary wound healing and drawing agents wherever we travel. Plantain spit poultice (leaves chewed in the mouth and then spit onto a wound) is the supreme remedy for a nettle sting.
- Tincture
- Oil/salve

Horsetail herb — Look for horsetail in wet and disturbed environments. Horsetail is loaded with silica and is supportive of overall tissue health.
- Dry for infusions — Water is the best menstruum, or solvent, to extract the silica content.
- Tincture — Works too.

Pine and fir needles — High in vitamin C and other immune-stimulating decongestant compounds. Nibble on these aromatic and sour wonders while on woodland forays.
- Dry for infusions

Uva ursi leaf — Harvest these leaves to help treat urinary tract infections.
- Dry for infusions
- Tincture

Mullein leaf — Growing in disturbed areas, harvest the leaves in their first year of growth for an excellent respiratory decongestant, lung tonic, and healer.
- Dry for infusions & smoke blends
- Tincture

In the Garden

Lemon balm leaf — This delicious and aromatic member of the mint family makes an excellent nervine, mood-lifter, and antiviral. Very easy to grow. Tends to take over.
- Dry for infusions
- Tincture
- Glycerite

Lady's mantle leaf — This magical alchemist's ally of a plant is a female reproductive tonic, pelvic decongestant, astringent, and very protective of the feminine spirit. My daughter's favorite plant.
- Dry for infusions
- Tincture

Feverfew leaf — The herbal remedy for sufferers of migraines. Also provides general headache and pain support. Bitter liver stimulant.
- Tincture

Garden sage leaf — Delicious culinary staple and wonderful to have in the garden for sore throats, colds, and flus.
- Dry for infusions & culinary spice
- Tincture

Horehound herb — A lesser-known member of the mint family that is easy to grow and a great cough remedy.
- Tincture
- Glycerite for children

Chapter 5:
Summer

Summer Spirit Walk

Let's take a walk on a beautiful, sunny summer morning.

As we step outside, the Sun's healing rays warm up our skin. We feel a rush of excitement in our hearts and a brightening of our spirits, for as the Sun shines it reflects the shine we feel inside: the desire to get out there and live, to be beautiful, and to "in-joy" the blessing of being alive. All of this courses through our veins as we close our eyes and breathe in the goodness of the moment.

Life is good. Life is light. All that exists is this present moment—and that is the blessing of life and the medicine of summer.

We've only just begun savoring the goodness of the Sun's healing before more excitement catches us. The roses have bloomed! There they are, fractaling, unfurling spirals of pure divine Creation with an aroma that is no less than the scent of the heavens. We bury our faces in the petals, inhaling deeply. How does the Creator accomplish this feat of beauty, we wonder?

As the scent of rose divinity wafts through our consciousness, we feel our higher spiritual centers blossoming open. "Yes, dear ones, I am beautiful," our minds hear rose say. "And you are too! You are the divine dance of Creation unfurling herself and you too are this holy, sacred expression of

Creation. Don't let the thorns of life distract you from this remembering, for the thorns are an essential part of the beauty too. You must accept and be the beauty when the beauty is present as it is here and now."

Our hearts open so wide from the downpour of spirit energy the rose unlocked that a tear of divine overwhelm falls from our eyes. "Life is good. I am beautiful. This is so," we hear as our hearts remember the great gift we are given to be alive on this Earth and the pleasure of being alive floods our cells.

"Thank you, elder sister, for this healing," our hearts beam to the roses. "How can we give back?"

"BE the BEAUTY that you are!" she responds. "Shine bright, no matter what. Share your beauty in this world. That is, in fact, why you are here."

We close our eyes and breathe with rose, exchanging our heart energy in a moment of pure sensual presence.

Summer Spirit Medicine

Summer is a time for be-ing. Summer is the time to revel in the raw experience of life at its fullest, the time for shining and sharing all that we are. Summer is for dancing, playing, singing, expressing, celebrating, and ritualizing the goodness of life. Summer is the time for being present with what is, embodying fully all that is within us, while we drink deeply of life's blossoming all around us.

Summer is a time of fertility. Biologically speaking, plants make flowers in order to reproduce. Flowers encase the reproductive structures of the plants. In a very real sense, plants make flowers in the hopes of getting laid! The plants have evolved the breathtaking beauty, intricate designs, and intoxicating aromas of their flowers as a means to attract pollinators as pollination ensures the continuation of their offspring. The energy of fertility permeates all of nature during the summer season, for plants and humans alike. Flowers reflect to us the medicine and importance of passion, pleasure, sensual delight, sexuality, and fertile creative energy.

Summer is a time of abundance. In summer there's an abundance of life-giving energy, an abundance of food from the Earth, and healing medicines in our gardens. Summer is a time when life is flowering and the beauty is spilling over to be shared and enjoyed by all. Our job is to enjoy it, receive it, create it, and be it! Summer is a time to be in the flow of the abundance of nature, participating in the receiving, the embodying, and the sharing of that generative flow.

Summer is a time of beauty. Is there anything in this Creation more breathtaking than flowers? Flowers are the peak expression of a plant's beauty. Gazing upon a flowering landscape is endlessly awe-inspiring and heart-opening. The fact that nature created these divine expressions is nothing short of miraculous. When we are in our most creative, beautiful, and authentic self-expression, we are in our flowering nature, the highest expression of all that we are—the flower in us. That is our beauty. That is Beauty. That is Being Beautiful. Flowers reflect this flowering aspect of our own nature, teaching us the importance of embodying our own beauty.

I was given a dream a few years back in which a wise inner teacher said to me plainly and clearly, "You know, daughter, striving is essential to keeping beauty alive." At the time of the dream and since its reception, the message of the dream comes when I feel my creativity wane or feel inner or outer voices holding me back from sharing my authentic expression. This dream was a gift from the flowering forces of life to my flowering nature. The plants have to *strive* to flower. It is hard work to make all that gorgeous! That striving and hard work are essential for keeping beauty alive—for them, for us, and for all of life.

Summer Spirit Medicine Reflections

Find a spot in nature where your eyes and heart are inspired and expanded by the sights of summer's floral beauty. Perhaps this is at the feet of a rose bush, in a wildflower meadow, a stand of yarrow, a bed of calendula, or anywhere the flowers are painting their colors upon the Earth. Dance the following questions around your mind-heart space.

* What is the inner beauty that I am?
* How does my beauty want to shine into this world?
* How am I expressing my beauty, my creativity, and my authenticity?
* What is my relationship with loving myself and loving all of life?
* How could I be more beautiful, authentic, and creative?
* How might these expressions serve all of Creation?

* How can I give back to feed all of life?

What Is Beauty?

Let's reclaim the notion of "beauty" from the homogenized and patriarchal confines of the dominant culture and try to seek out its original nature. What is beauty? What would the flowers say if we were to pose this question to them? They might respond with something like this…

* Beauty is that which creates life.

* Beauty is that which feeds life.

* Beauty is that which inspires life.

* Beauty is that which opens the heart.

* Beauty is that which dances and inspires dances.

* Beauty generates, gives, inspires, feeds, and thinks beyond oneself.

* Beauty has zero to do with specific metrics of physical attractiveness and everything to do with individuality, uniqueness, authenticity, and creativity.

* Beauty blossoms from the inside.

* The outer is the expression of the inner and in that expression, beauty feeds and inspires beauty to grow outside of itself.

The truest definition of beauty I'm aware of is from Martín Prechtel, author and voice for the indigenous heart, when he described the beauty of a Mayan goddess.

" . . . what the world remembered was her beauty. She was not just beautiful like some people think of beautiful, for her beauty was not just for herself. It was the kind of beauty that didn't kill or isolate. She made everything and everyone that saw her or that she saw, touched, or walked over want to live a little longer just from the hope of seeing her again. The world flowered and grew wherever she passed. When she brushed by them, wild orchids and lilies mutated into forms and colors never seen before. Even rocks would sparkle, split, and crumble into smaller chunks, then grow their ecstatic fragments back into cliffs, defying time and geology, and all because they felt her sueded feet step upon them."[1]

Summer Herbalism

The beauty and splendor of summer are most fully expressed in the flowering plants and this—the flowers—is the herbalism of the summer season.

Flowers are at their peak potency when harvested early in the morning, shortly after sunrise, and on a dry day. At this time, their opening blossoming energies are strongest as the Sun's energies pull them into their beautiful unfurled radiance. The earlier in the season, or the closer the harvest is to when the flowers first appeared, also usually makes for a potent harvest. As soon as the buds start to brown or wither, peak potency has passed. You will notice some flowers in the following section, such as hawthorn, St. John's wort, and yarrow, are considered peak when some of the buds are still closed and some have popped open.

Summer is also the time to make flower essences, for the simple reason that the flowers are seasonally available.

Essences are a lovely way to capture the spirit medicine of a plant. It comes as no surprise that they are predominately made from flowers, for flowers are believed to be the peak expression of a plant's life cycle. Flower essences are a vibrational imprint of the energy of a flower held within water, ingested by us to awaken our own flowering nature, to shift, unlock, and elevate us into higher and more radiant states of spirit. Flower essences are powerful and relatively easy to create. They are like summer in a bottle. See page 253 for instructions.

WILD ROSE
Rosa nutkana and *Rosa gymnocarpa*

Note: These two rose species are the indigenous roses of the Pacific Northwest and can be worked with interchangeably. Thankfully, the following medicinal information can be applied to cultivated roses as well. If they look and smell like roses, they carry the medicine below.

Body Parts: Flower petals

Other Parts at Other Times of Year:
* Fall — Harvest the hips (see page 167)

Harvesting: Wild roses have much daintier flowers than their cultivated counterparts. Their floral bodies are made of five soft, perfect petals and it's these petals that are the medicine. Hand-pluck the petals straight into a harvesting basket.

Rose has vitamin C. Rose petals contain good amounts of vitamin C, making them a powerhouse of healing for the skin, heart, and immune system.

Rose is astringent and cooling on the inside. Rose petals are healing and soothing to red, inflamed tissues. They can be prepared as an infusion and utilized as a mouth rinse for sores, bleeding gums, and mouth ulcers, and as a gargle for irritated sore throats.

Rose is astringent and cooling on the outside. Topically, rose petals are simply splendid at cooling off the heat and inflammation from sunburns, rashes, and red skin irritations. Homemade rose water or liniment is a wonderful toner for the skin and is suitable for all skin types. Topical application of rose also helps to heal, soothe, and prevent acne.

Rose loves the heart. Rose is a nervine that helps to soothe, heal, and restore the health of nervous system tissues. The plant has a special affinity for the heart. Consider adding rose petals to teas and tinctures for frayed nerves and emotional challenges that could use some heart-soothing, heart-cooling, and heart-opening medicine.

Rose loves the womb. Rose is a uterine tonic and pelvic decongestant. Consider adding rose to formulas for improved pelvic and reproductive health, including menstrual challenges, fertility, libido, and blocked creative flow.

Rose reflects our divine nature. There is a Catholic belief that the scent of rose is proof that God loves us. That's the closest we might come to describing the spirit medicine of rose with

English words. We see roses associated with divine goddesses the world over. Mother Mary in the Christian tradition, Venus in the Greek tradition, and Isis in the Egyptian tradition are just a few of the rose lineup. Similar to the lotus flower in the Hindu tradition, rose is emblematic of "the perfected soul." The perfection of divinity. The highest harmonic of embodied expression. The vibration of love. That which is our truest divine nature that our human lives are in a process of re-membering. Rose awakens this very divinity.

Rose reflects beauty. Rose teaches us that all love arises from self-love and that beauty blossoms from within. Rose shows us how to be the beauty that we are, the unique expression of a rippling vibration of Creation. Rose reminds us that we are here for nothing other than to express our blossoming. When we are the beauty that we were made to be, we inspire that beauty in others and raise the vibration of all of Creation around us.

Rose teaches us to plant seeds of beauty. Though I have always loved and admired roses, it wasn't until many years into our relationship that the bond between rose and I really blossomed. While preparing for an herb class one evening, I received a message from Spirit loud and clear, saying, "Daughter! You must put rose in every offering blend, on every altar, that you create. The Earth needs seeds of beauty." It felt like an important request coming through on a loudspeaker. I have heeded the request since, always including rose petals in any offering that I make to the Earth or altar I create. In a time of spiraling confusion, delusion, darkness, and chaos, rose has quite literally been a lifeline of doing-being-planting what really matters: beauty. May we all be seed-planters of beauty.

Rose heals our hearts. Rose softens, cools, opens, nurtures, and *loves* a tense, grieving, and broken heart. She is like a hug from Mother Divine herself. Work with rose when we need to remember the beauty in life because we have temporarily forgotten due to heartbreak or hope-break.

Rose teaches us about paradox. The most exquisitely soft flowers and the gnarliest of thorns—rose thoroughly embodies this paradox of being open and receptive while protected and fierce. Rose holds the imprint of "the sacred marriage within," or the integration of opposites.

I received the following dream the night before hosting a blessing way for a friend preparing to have her first child. A blessing way is a woman-centered ceremony for pregnant mamas-to-be with the purpose of blessing, honoring, and preparing the woman to give birth to her baby and herself as a mother. In the dream, I saw my friend, full-belly pregnant and all, inside of a rose flower. As I gazed upon my beautiful friend inside a rose flower, rose was teaching me. She said, "Childbirth is about becoming one with the rose. Women must become as soft, tender, and open as the petals of a rose, surrendering to become as fierce as the thorns the flower possesses." I couldn't imagine a more perfect image or teacher for the juxtaposition of ferocity and surrender required to birth a child into this world. By the way, my friend loved her childbirth experience and is flowering in her motherhood.

Dry for infusions — Rose plays beautifully with others in tea blends and a little goes a long way. Consider adding rose petals to tea formulas for stress and mood support, sleep support, and any physical challenge of a sacred feminine nature.

Dry for bath blends — Bathing in rose helps reconnect us to the beauty of our own nature and the beauty of life. When our spirits need an uplift or our hearts need a cleanse, a rose spirit bath can be just the remedy.

Liniment — Infuse the petals in witch hazel extract, available from any drug store, then prepare as we would a tincture. This liniment is most excellent to have around in case of sunburns, burns, rashes, and all manner of red-hot skin challenges.

Dry for offerings — If we work with a lot of roses, then we might consider using *wild* rose petals for elixirs and special occasion tea blends and using *cultivated* roses for other purposes. Cultivated roses are plentiful in commerce, allowing us to lighten the load on wild populations.

Herbal Formula: Wild Rose Elixir

This way of making a tincture has just a few extra steps and is incredibly worth it. It's delicious. The use of heat to make an infusion of the petals, plus the brandy and the honey, makes it a divine elixir indeed.

1 cup fresh wild rose petals
Mason jar with lid
¼ cup water
½ cup honey
½ cup brandy

Place wild rose petals in a Mason jar. Boil and pour the hot water over the petals. Cover the jar with its lid and let the petals steam for 5 minutes. After 5 minutes, add the honey and brandy and then replace the lid. Let steep for 2 weeks, then strain.

This elixir can be sipped as-is, taken as a simple, or added to formulas.

Other Formulas:
Womb Love Tea page 101
Tincture for the Grouchies page 123
Flowering Nature Tea page 133
Heart Hug Tincture page 166

ST. JOHN'S WORT
Hypericum perforatum

Body Parts: Leaves and flowers

Harvesting: Right around the summer solstice, or St. John's Day, for whom the plant is named, is St. John's wort harvesting time. It is prime when the yellow flower buds just begin to burst open into their flowering, with half of the flowers open in full bloom and half still closed in their buds. Use snips or scissors to snip off these flowers and buds plus 1 to 2 inches of the nearby leaves, making certain to harvest before the flowers are pollinated and begin to look brown and dried out.

Safety: St. John's wort interacts with many pharmaceutical drugs, including birth control pills and certain antibiotics and antidepressants, among others. If taking any pharmaceuticals, consult with a health care provider to determine if there are herb-drug interactions before ingesting this plant.

St. John's wort is nerve medicine. St. John's wort has a very special affinity for the nerves and is a nervine par excellence. Deeply restorative, regenerative, and healing to nerve tissues, St. John's wort is excellent both internally and externally when there is nerve inflammation or nerve damage. The plant has a special ability for healing deep burns.

St. John's wort is pain medicine. St. John's wort has analgesic pain-relieving properties that have a general body-wide effect. That affinity to the nerves makes the plant a specific remedy for nerve pains like back spasms, neck cramps, neuralgias, and sciatica.

St. John's wort fights viruses. As a reliable anti-viral, St. John's wort is excellent medicine for viral infections that live in the nerves and cause pain, such as herpes, shingles, and Epstein-Barr.

St. John's wort heals tissues. Often included in all-purpose topical skin salves, St. John's wort is a wonderful vulnerary, or skin-healing herb, that helps skin tissue heal, repair, and regenerate.

St. John's wort brightens the mood. And then there is what many know St. John's wort for: depression. While it's not a one-size-fits-all for folks with depression, in the right situations for the right people with the right kind of depression, St. John's wort can be magical. The plant is like liquid sunshine to the soul and spirit. As master herbalist Michael Moore so aptly put it, St. John's wort "has little or no value in bipolar depression or depressive states with a clear pathology. It is for normal folks whose strategies have failed and are temporarily adrift."[2] For folks with mild to moderate depression, St. John's wort can sincerely help restore the spirit and ease depressive feelings. The plant is specifically helpful for a "case of the grouchies" often occurring in PMS, seasonal affective disorder (SAD), or simply a touch of the winter blues.

St. John's wort lets the light in. Sacred to the Sun, St. John's wort shines and grows the energy of the Sun in the body and the spirit. Anytime we find ourselves in a situation of having lost the light—perhaps losing hope, losing joy, losing the will to live, or losing a grip—think of St. John's wort. The loss of light might manifest as depression, grouchiness, despair, or deep frustration. St. John's wort reflects the energy of the Sun straight back into the lost spirit to "let the light back in," reconnecting us to the bright, sunny light of our soul nature.

St. John's wort is protective. St. John's wort provides powerful spiritual protection. Often hung over doorways, near the bed, or worn on the body, St. John's wort protects from the influences of negative energies. The plant accomplishes this by connecting us so deeply to our own light that we become impenetrable fortresses. With so much light coursing through the spirit and the space, no darkness can grow.

St. John's wort protects the feminine spirit. Dr. Deborah "Dancing Crow" Frances, a well-known herbalist and Lakota elder, says, "St. John's wort's spiritually protective qualities have a special affinity for the reproductive tract. Recognizing that women are more sensitive and open during their menses, women in traditional cultures in Europe painted their labia with an oil of St. John's wort for protection during moontime."[3] St. John's wort protects the pelvic bowls, vulvas, and uteruses of the world. Though the flowers are yellow, medicinal preparations of this plant are a deep red color that looks strikingly like menstrual blood. Applying this deep-red infused oil topically to the lower belly provides a profoundly effective layer of protection. Consider doing this when bleeding or every day all month long to protect and connect to the power of the feminine light within while navigating invasive energies.

Note: St. John's wort is a plant that is much more potent fresh than dried. Consider this when making the preparations below.

Tincture — Process the tincture of flowers and leaflets immediately upon harvesting. If the preparation turns a bright red color, it's a good sign the medicine will be strong. This tincture can be taken singly or added to blends for mood balance, sleep support, menstrual discomforts, viral challenges, and spirit elevation.

Infused oil — Process the fresh leaves and flowers into an infused oil and consider applying it every day as an empowering protection for the pelvic bowl, womb, and vulva.

Salve — Add beeswax and whip into a salve (see page 248) to serve as an all-purpose skin healer for scrapes, bites, stings, rashes, bumps, bruises, and all varieties of ouchies.

Dry for infusions — Though not the most delicious-tasting tea, St. John's wort does play nicely with other more tasty nervine herbs. It's a great herb to have around for tea formulations.

Herbal Formula: Tincture for the Grouchies

This blend is for regular people who have become a bit knocked off balance mood-wise and can't shake it. It helps "let the light back in," soothe the nerves, and restore us to the flow of life-giving-life energy.

Prepare a tincture of equal parts of the following fresh or dried herbs.

St. John's wort leaf and flower
Hawthorn berry
Lemon balm leaf
Wild rose petal

Directions: Consider taking 1 to 2 droppersful 3x daily.

Other Formulas:
Skin-Healer Salve page 87
Spirit Reset Bath page 138
Empowered Tincture page 155
Trauma Salve page 209

YARROW
Achillea spp.

Body Parts: Flowers

Other Parts at Other Times:
* Spring or Summer — Snip the leaves.
* Fall or Winter — Dig up the roots.

Harvesting: Use snips or scissors to snip off the flowering heads. They're at peak potency when some of the flowers are still closed in buds and some have popped open into full flowering. If they smell strong, beautiful, and like yarrow, then it's the right time.

Safety: Not safe for use during pregnancy.

Yarrow does it all. If stranded on a desert island and only allowed to choose one plant, I would bring yarrow. Yarrow's Latin name, *Achillea,* pays homage to the famous Greek demigod warrior Achilles who, until his fatal Achilles tendon injury, was unstoppable on the battlefield. The legend states that his success in battle was due to his use of yarrow and the plant's magical ability to heal all inflicted wounds.

Yarrow arrests bleeding. As a styptic, yarrow generally helps to arrest bleeding. Yarrow slows the bleeding of external wounds and is an invaluable first aid and wound care remedy. Yarrow even helps to slow nosebleeds.

Yarrow tonifies the womb. Yarrow has a balancing and restoring effect on the womb. If there is stagnation, yarrow tends to increase circulation and promote menstrual flow. If there is excess bleeding, yarrow tends to staunch and slow bleeding, restoring tone to boggy tissue. Yarrow is a wonderful ally to the womb postpartum and can even help in cases of prolapse.

Yarrow is anti-inflammatory. Loaded with anti-inflammatory essential oil compounds, yarrow brings healing to bruising, swelling, and injuries. The flowers are a most excellent mover of stagnant blood and are often added to topical anti-inflammatory salves and oils for general bump and bruise support.

Yarrow is a cold and flu remedy. Being very diaphoretic, blood-moving, and antiseptic, yarrow tea is an amazing cold and flu remedy, helping support the body when moving through fever.

Yarrow is protective. Yarrow is a powerfully protective plant, reflecting to us the righteousness of our own warrior nature when we might be struggling with standing in our power. Yarrow helps sensitive, empathic folks who might become overwhelmed or overstimulated by the energies or people in their environments. Yarrow helps to repair the auric shields in our energetic fields, making us less permeable and affected by the circumstances around us. For folks who feel overwhelmed by a crowd, swamped by the toxicity of a work environment, slimed after time with someone in a bad mood, or anything similar, yarrow helps awaken the righteous boundaries needed to fully inhabit ourselves and increase our feelings of resilience and protection.

Though it's hard to believe now, there was a short time in my life when I was plagued by public speaking anxiety. The moment I stood to speak, my chest and throat would flood with energy, causing my heart to race and my throat to close. It was a near panic attack.

I went to the plants for help and yarrow stepped forward in my aid. Yarrow shared with me its medicine of creating a shield around the energy body so that I could be and speak within my own energy field. I wore a bit of yarrow in a medicine bag and took a few minutes to connect with the warrior shield of yarrow before speaking engagements.

Though I still felt the huge rush of energy, it didn't penetrate into my body so deeply as to affect my physiology. I was able to speak. As I've continued to deepen my relationship with the plant, I've come to understand more about what was happening to me. When in a group setting in the position of being the speaker, there is a lot of energy circulating in the room. People's anxiety, excitement—there's a palpable energetic tension. Being quite sensitive and empathic, it was my perception of this energy field, rather than my own authentic anxiety, that was flooding and crippling me.

By working with yarrow, I realized that I could be in this field of group tension and not be consumed by it. Instead I could be protected in my own space so that I could show up and speak in and from my warrior nature. As someone whose destiny has involved quite a lot of public speaking, this healing that yarrow granted me was a big little miracle.

Yarrow aids the wounded healer. For those brave-tender souls who work in healing arenas of all kinds, yarrow helps keep the heart open to the warrior's work that is healing. The plant helps foster our resilience to sit in and with the suffering fields of others and our planet. Yarrow mirrors the strength and endurance to stay fiercely open-hearted, strongly loving, and endlessly compassionate, even in the midst of all the suffering we interface with at this time on this planet. Call on yarrow when compassion fatigue is creeping in or the weights of the world are weighing too heavily. Yarrow will call you back to action.

Tincture — Keep tincture on hand for all kinds of internal needs. Remember yarrow is a panacea and will find its way into many formulas for internal support and treatment. Consider working with yarrow tincture often as drop dosing when in need of some extra spiritual support and protection.

Dry for infusions — Helpful for all the things, but perhaps most especially as a diaphoretic tea for fevers, colds, and flus, yarrow tea is one to have in the medicine cabinet.

Infused oil — An excellent all-purpose topical for infections, scrapes, bumps, bruises, and owies of all kinds, it's hard to think of a topical oil or salve in which yarrow wouldn't earn a place on the ingredient list. Yarrow is also a most excellent anointing oil when one is integrating spiritual protection or boundaries.

Herbal Formula: Cold and Flu Care Tea

Note: I did not create this formula. It is an old European folk formula for supporting the body through fevers and providing antiviral support in fighting off a cold or flu. Consider keeping this blend in the family's herbal cupboard for seasonal respiratory challenges.

Mix together equal parts of the following dried herbs.

Yarrow flower
Peppermint leaf
Elderflower

Steep 4 tablespoons per quart of water for 15 minutes. Strain and sip throughout the day when fighting a cold or flu.

Other Formulas:
Spirit Reset Bath page 138
Empowered Tincture page 155
Urinary Soother Drops page 160

CALENDULA
Calendula spp.

Body Parts: Flowers

Growing and Harvesting: Calendula doesn't grow wild in North America, but boy does it like to grow here. Once established in a yard or garden, this annual will self-seed and return year after year. Calendula is a delight to have in the garden and not just because it is so easy to grow. Use snips or scissors to snip off the flowers when they appear. It's best to snip some off every day when flowering as this encourages more flowering and will increase the harvest.

Calendula heals the skin. Calendula is the supreme vulnerary, skin-healing herb. Topical application of the flowers brings healing to skin complaints, such as rashes, scrapes, bites, burns, cuts, wounds, and all manner of skin ouchies. Calendula soothes, cools, disinfects, and heals skin tissues.

Calendula heals the inner skin. When taken internally, calendula has the same effects as it does on the outer skin. The tissues that line the respiratory, digestive, vaginal, and urinary tracts all benefit from calendula's demulcent, or soothing, effect. Calendula can soothe a sore throat, soothe an inflamed urinary tract or vagina, and soothe irritated digestive tissues, such as those resulting from diarrhea, heartburn, or IBS-type symptoms.

Calendula is antifungal. Somewhat surprisingly, calendula's skin-healing softness is accompanied by some kickass resins that give these flowers a unique antifungal effect. They can be helpful for all kinds of internal fungal challenges, such as candida overgrowth, vaginal yeast, and thrush.

Calendula loves the children. Calendula is one of those plants with a special affinity for the little ones, perhaps because they are so bright, beautiful, and soothing. Calendula is amazing for diaper rashes, eczemas, rashes, bug bites, dermatitis, and all manner of itchy skin kid stuff. As an antifungal, calendula is supreme for shifting the internal fungal ecology in the little ones.

Calendula softens the spirit. Calendula reflects to us the possibility of being soft, warm, abundant, generous, and beautiful in our beingness. The absolute ease and grace with which calendula grows reminds us of the benevolence of the Universe and of Life. Calendula reminds us that we can release stories telling us that "things are so hard" and return to a state of purity and childlike delight.

Calendula brightens the spirit. Calendula helps to alleviate depression and hopeless despair and is a beautiful remedy for a case of the blues.

Calendula was in the Garden of Eden. Innocence, light, and the vibration of abundance—a garden peppered with calendula flowers automatically brightens the spirit and restores a sense of hope to a dampened spirit. Calendula whispered to me once, "I was in the Garden of Eden." As I looked closer with my inner eye, I saw and felt in calendula the vibration of an abundant and generous flowering Earth oozing off its flowers—the very spirit of the Garden of Eden. Calendula's seeds are shaped like a crescent Moon. New Moon energy is innocent, young, pure, hopeful, expansive, and generative. Sit with calendula to restore these abundances to the spirit.

Infused oil/salve — By far, the way I work with calendula most is as an infused oil that is then turned into a salve. To make the infused oil, consider doing a quick-dry of the calendula flowers. After harvest, lay them out on a sheet, towel, or drying rack for just a night or two. This quick-dry removes a good amount of the moisture content but still retains much of the fresh potency and life force. These flowers are then infused into olive oil. Adding beeswax turns the oil into a salve.

Tincture — Infuse the flowers fresh into alcohol to have tincture on hand for sore throats and digestive upsets.

Dry for infusions and baths — In addition to the myriad medicinal benefits, the dried flowers make teas and bath blends more beautiful to admire. A favorite bath herb.

Herbal Formula: Flowering Nature Tea

This is an all-flower tea, with the exception of lemon balm, designed to support and nourish our own flowering nature. It's delicate, delicious, and beautiful.

Blend the following dried herbs together.

¼ ounce calendula flower
¼ ounce lavender flower
½ ounce chamomile flower
½ ounce lemon balm herb
½ ounce red clover flower
½ ounce wild rose petal

Steep 4 tablespoons in a quart of water for 15 minutes. Strain and drink throughout the day. Serve hot or cold.

Other Formulas:
Skin-Healer Salve page 87
Fight the Fungus Salve page 188

SELF-HEAL
Prunella vulgaris

Body Parts: Aerial parts when flowering

Harvesting: Self-heal can be found growing in lawns, gardens, and meadowy areas. Use snips or scissors to hand-mow the aboveground parts of the plant, including stems, leaves, and flowers.

Self-heal cleanses. This lovely, hardy herb is often overlooked amongst modern herbalists, even though it is readily found and available. Like many of its weedy relatives, such as cleavers and chickweed, self-heal ranks amongst the blood-cleansing alteratives, plants that help aid the body's detoxification pathways. The plant is bitter and thus inspires in the human body all the benefits of bitters, including improved detoxification, circulation, and overall cleansing. The old texts describe self-heal as helpful in rheumatism and arthritis due to this cleansing and anti-inflammatory cooling effect.

Self-heal heals the body. Self-heal is a wound healer extraordinaire, an excellent ally to keep on hand for first aid skin afflictions of all kinds. As an astringent, self-heal helps to arrest bleeding, tone and tighten the tissues, and fight infection. As a vulnerary, the plant is soothing and healing to wounds of all kinds, aiding in tissue repair, and cools and soothes irritated and inflamed tissues. This plant undoubtedly deserves a place in skin-healing, first aid, and all-purpose salves. Due to properties that aid in healing the tissues inside of the body as well, self-heal is not to be overlooked for inclusion in formulas for digestive and respiratory health.

Self-heal fights viruses. This lovely, humble herb packs an antiviral punch, effective against many viruses, including herpes, the flu, and the common cold. For folks with chronic or acute herpes, self-heal certainly deserves a spot in internal and topical herbal preparations to treat or prevent lesions. At the first sign of a cold or flu and during recovery, self-heal is a good one to consider to prevent viral spread and to get the lymphatic system on board. Self-heal has an affinity for the lymph. When fighting or recovering from infection, the extra lymph-stimulating property goes a long way toward helping the body heal.

Self-heal heals the spirit. One of the best-selling and most widely used flower essences of all time, self-heal has been taken by millions of folks over the past few decades to help them *heal* from all manner of physical and spiritual challenges. Flower essences are herbal preparations that hold the vibrational imprint of a plant spirit. As its name suggests, self-heal holds, reflects, and awakens the vibration of *healing*.

All of life is constantly on a journey of healing, of whole-ing, of recovery, of integration, of re-incorporation, and of seeking a return to a state of homeostasis. Self-heal holds and embodies the vibration of this healing force, the "vis" as naturopathic doctors call it, "chi" as it's named in Traditional Chinese Medicine, or "prana" as described in the yogic tradition. Self-heal stimulates the body's natural healing mechanism, or life force, to heal that which has fallen out of the balanced and whole vital state.

When working through a challenging soul process, such as trauma recovery or a broken heart and its downstream effects, consider including self-heal. I include self-heal in healing ceremonies of all kinds, for all manner of soul and body afflictions, because the plant catalyzes, or *potentizes*, the life force to heal. When we're bogged down by physical health constraints, such as chronic disease, chronic fatigue, weakened vitality, or weakened immunity, self-heal can help catalyze our vitality to regain more life force.

Self-heal has this effect on our mental, psychic, and emotional spheres as well. Whenever we have become aware enough of a pattern that we can name it and name that we want to shift it, bringing self-heal in helps to move our energies toward that healed and whole state.

Dry for infusions — Consider adding self-heal to tea blends for both physical and spiritual healing. The plant is safe to take in tonic amounts and has a mild flavor that plays well with others. Plus, the dried flowers are beautiful!

Dry for bath blends — Incorporate self-heal into bath blends for all manner of spiritual bathing ceremonies. The plant is incredibly powerful in its ability to potentize healing.

Tincture — Include the tincture in formulas for soul-healing and heart-healing as well as for its detoxification, antiviral, and anti-inflammatory properties.

Other Formulas:
Skin-Healer Salve page 87
Trauma Salve page 209

Herbal Formula: Spirit Reset Bath

This spiritual bath helps to cleanse, invigorate, and heal the spirit. We all have those times when we just feel a bit "off," as though we picked something up, can't shake an energy, or are just in deep need of a healing reset. In these instances, healing herbal baths are invaluable and incredibly effective at resetting the spirit.

Prepare a blend of equal parts of the following herbs, fresh or dried.

Self-heal aerial part
Wild rose petal
Yarrow flower
Red cedar leave
If you have it, add in a handful of white or desert sage.
If you have it, add 2 cups of Epsom salt to the bathwater.

Tie a large handful of the herbs into a ball of cheesecloth or place them in a muslin bag. Boil a big pot of water (a 2- to 3-gallon pot if you have one). Once boiling, remove from heat and toss the bundle of herbs into the water. Let it steep, covered, for at least 30 minutes. In the meantime, draw a bath. Once the bath is drawn and the herbs have steeped, pour the tea into the bathwater along with 2 cups of Epsom salts if available. Check the temperature to make sure it's not too hot, then climb in and let the healing plants soak away the energetic muck, reset, and heal the spirit. The experience is nothing short of divine.

Going Deeper into Summer

In the Wild
California poppy — Growing all over the West Coast, harvest the whole plant when flowering, roots and all. California poppy loves kids of all ages, relieves pain and stress, and supports sleep.
- * Tincture
- * Glycerite for children
- * Dry for infusions

Elderflower— For more on the medicine of elder, see page 170. The flowers come before the berries and are a reliable diaphoretic and support for fevers and flus.
- * Dry for infusions
- * Tincture

Mullein flower — Found in most disturbed areas, these yellow flowers are incredibly healing to the nerves. They decrease pain and help heal ear infections.
- * Infused oil — Infuse with garlic and St. John's wort for an ear infection oil.
- * Tincture — For nerve support formulas.

Red clover flower — Growing in most disturbed or cultivated areas, these flowers are alterative, nutritive, antioxidant, and balancing to the female reproductive system.
- * Dry for infusions
- * Tincture

Wild bleeding heart — Note: Low-dose plant; only ingest under supervision. Harvest the whole plant when flowering, roots and all, from woodland meadows. This low-dose plant has pain-relieving and trauma-healing effects and is a powerful healer of the spiritual heart.
* Flower essence — For the spiritual heart properties.
* Tincture — Taken as a low-dose with medical guidance for pain relief.

In the Garden

Chamomile flower — Incredibly easy to grow, this self-seeding annual will come back year after year. A staple in the home herbal garden for soothing and calming the nerves, minds, and tummies of all ages.
* Dry for infusions
* Tincture
* Glycerite for children

Motherwort flowering aerial parts — This mint family member grows easily without a lot of fuss. Harvest the aerial parts when in flower for nerve, heart, and female reproductive support.
* Tincture
* Dry for infusions

Skullcap flowering aerial parts — Another mint-family member that is easy to grow. Harvest aerial parts when flowering. Reliable nervine, pain reliever, mood balancer, and sleep supporter.
* Tincture
* Dry for infusions

Arnica flowers — Note: This plant is NOT SAFE for internal use and should only be used topically. Invited from the alpine meadows into the garden, arnica flower relieves pain, supports healing, and blunts the effects of trauma of all kinds.
- Infused oil/salves — Topical for healing all traumas.
- Flower essence — Arnica is too toxic for internal use without medical guidance, though the flower essence works wonders and is safe.

Lavender flowers — Lavender promotes sleep, eases feelings of depression, balances mood, and soothes the spirit.
- Tincture
- Glycerite
- Dry for infusions
- Dry for baths

Chapter 6: Fall

Fall Spirit Walk

Autumn often creeps up on us unexpectedly. We were so busy being present and beautiful and in-joy during the summer, it can feel as though it all passed by in the blink of an eye.

Unlike the seasons past, while heading outside, we will want to put on long sleeves and a hat as mornings have started to become brisk. We feel the knocking of autumn's chill and the rise of the call to turn within. The knock causes a simultaneous wave of grief and sigh of relief to emerge from the door of our hearts. We are standing on the threshold between times on the wheel of the year.

Walking outside, it's apparent that we are not quite out of summer yet. There are still green leaves, fruits, and even flowers to be seen! But the gravitational pull within has entered the atmosphere and as it stirs within we can feel that the darker times are just around the corner, pulling us inward.

We head out for a walk through the woods. We see that leaves have begun falling from the trees and again that dual wave of grief and sigh of relief flood side-by-side from our hearts. Our walk through the woods reveals plant life in many stages of growth. The late summer berries are still out so we stop and munch on a few huckleberries and blueberries, making sure to save some for the bears and the birds.

Seeing and consuming these woodland berries reminds us of our seasonal medicinal to-dos. We note that it's time to go check on our favorite hawthorn grove and to plan the day of the elderberry harvest.

We continue walking through the woods, reflecting on that stir of grief/relief that is swirling in an alchemy that we can't yet define in our hearts. We arrive at the devil's club patch, immediately noticing that the leaves on the devil's club have begun to brown and wither. Then we know without a doubt that fall is indeed here. Grief temporarily wins out over relief in our hearts as tears begin to fall from our eyes

"Come, sit with me," our wise grandfather the devil's club whispers as a knowing in our hearts. We approach, tears and all, not even really knowing why we are crying or what we are crying about, carefully and reverently moving our bodies to sit at the feet of this stand of forest elders.

"That grief that floods you, my child, that grief is life. Do not fight it. Let it course through you and wash away the burdens you needn't carry any longer. The wheel always turns. No summer can last forever. That would mean life would cease. Come sit, cry, and tell me about all you did and were these months past. And I will teach you about what it is to let go."

The grief floods our heart and as the tears fall, miraculously and surprisingly, the grief begins to give way to a sense of sweet relief. Relief that the gravitational pull within is actually here and that now for the next handful of months, we will dream more, write more, sleep more, and gestate more.

Devil's club reminds us that in no time at all, his body will look like nothing more than a stand of dried-out bones, barely even recognizable as life. "This is what will be happening to you as well, my children. Your bodies might not wear it as perceptibly as mine, but your souls will be bared down to bones. Let it happen. Don't fight it. Life will come again in the spring. But that is not this threshold. This threshold is the threshold to the darker times, the threshold that leads within."

We thank the devil's club and make our way to leave, promising that we will return in a few weeks' time when he has fully shapeshifted into the pregnant boneyard that is his winter body. For now though, as we are still in that threshold, the time betwixt and between, we remember that there is still much bounty to harvest from nature before true winter arrives.

Fall Spirit Medicine

Fall is a threshold. Like any threshold, this time on the wheel between summer's beauty and winter's descent is supercharged with a palpable kind of atmospheric pregnancy. It's as though all of nature, including ourselves, reflected by the plants, knows that change is here and coming. The magnetic pull of the call within is swirling within us, gravitationally whispering that it's almost time to pull our energy downward and inward. But the paradox of this threshold time is that even though that gravitational pull is in the atmosphere, when we open our eyes and look outside, abundance is still everywhere! Fall is a time of decay and of abundance. We truly stand betwixt and between.

Fall is a harvest time. This is the last of the harvest time. The time of gathering up the fruits of all that we have planted, tended, danced with, sung to, and enjoyed in summer. In the garden and in the wild, this is a time of busy harvesting. Within our own beings, fall is also the time to *harvest* all that we have learned, gained, obtained, and created during the previous growing times. It's a time to invite all of this to integrate into our beings.

Fall is a time of letting go. Being a threshold, fall is a time to let go of that which we have learned we no longer need. It's a time of shedding, of dying away, of letting our old leaves fall away to what wants to reemerge after the deep sleep/death of winter. It's the beginning of the turn within.

Fall Spirit Medicine Reflections

Find a spot in nature that stirs that paradoxical feeling of grief/relief within the heart. Perhaps it's a forest of deciduous trees where the forest floor is covered with fallen leaves yet some still remain on the trees. Perhaps it is in a meadow with abundantly berried hawthorn trees and the plants of the understory have started to fade and die back. Once you've found this spot, drop down and find "the fall within," letting the following questions enter into your heart and mind.

- What am I harvesting from this past year? What have I learned, assimilated, integrated, embodied, accomplished, achieved, and inner-stood?

- What in my nature or life is falling away so that I might more fully embody and inhabit these new harvests?

* How might these harvests serve all of Creation?

* What griefs am I the carrier of? Personal, ancestral, familial, communal, collective, planetary? What ceremonies are needed for these griefs to be properly honored?

* What dream-seeds am I carrying through this threshold to gestate through the coming winter?

* How can I give back to feed all of life?

Fall Herbalism

Fall is a time of duality, paradox, and threshold. We certainly see this reflected in the plant world. Many of the plants are at the peak of their bodies' physical strength (fruits). Yet just after that peak expresses itself, the whole plant begins to die back toward its underground hibernation.

Fruits — In early fall, herbalists are thinking about harvesting medicinal fruits at their time of peak potency, such as huckleberries and blueberries, hawthorn berries, elderberries, and rose hips.

Seeds — Fall is the time for harvesting medicinal seeds such as wild carrot, fennel, dill, nettle, and burdock as well as for harvesting and saving seeds from the plants we are cultivating in the garden.

Roots — When the plants begin to die back, we begin to think about harvesting roots, though we wait to do so as late in the season as possible before the ground enters into a hard freeze.

Barks — Medicinal barks, such as devil's club, alder, and willow, are often harvested in the fall once the life force begins to travel back underground for the winter.

DEVIL'S CLUB
Oplopanax horridus

Body Parts: Inner bark

Harvesting: It is absolutely essential to wear sturdy leather gloves when handling devil's club as getting pricked by the spines can cause a nasty dermatitis. What's more, the spines may contain *Staphylococcus* bacteria that can lead to severe skin infection. This is a plant to respect. Devil's club has a unique growth habit, growing in clusters or communities of intersecting plants. When the stems fall over, they become the new rhizomes for new shoots and stems to grow out of. Beginning at the outer edge of the stand, use gloved hands to gently tug on the rhizomes lying just under the layer of forest floor mulch. When one is found that stands between two stems and tugging on it reveals that the stems are pretty sturdy and likely won't tip over if the chunk of rhizome is removed, it's a good spot to harvest. Use loppers to remove the rhizome between the two vertical standing stems.

Garbling: Continue to wear leather gloves throughout the garbling process. Roots will have varying levels of spines on them depending on their age and other factors. Use the back end of a garbling knife and/or the rough side of a dry sponge to scrape away the spines. Next, use a garbling knife or dull paring knife to scrape off the root bark. The medicinally potent bark will look brown on one side and green on the other. Scraping off this bark will reveal a woody inner stick of the devil's club, which can be saved and used in a sacred manner.

Devil's club teaches stewardship. Devil's club is a powerful medicine who offers many unique and amazing medicinal actions in the human body. Among these are optimizing blood sugar levels and metabolism, improving stress resilience, decongesting the lungs and respiratory system, and balancing inflammation in the body. However, the more I have sat with devil's club, the more convinced I have become that the plant is special, sacred, and deserving of protection. I feel that devil's club should not be worked with for physical medicine other than in highly intentional and specific situations.

Even though devil's club has healthy populations currently, we all know that this abundance can change in a generation, a decade, or even a year. Let us practice cultivating our stewardship and integrity with this plant. Let's not overly harvest devil's club, instead taking only very small amounts in very intentional ways for very sacred purposes, working with devil's club only for spirit medicine. This means only small amounts are required, such as drop doses for tinctures or working with the dead sticks often found on the edge of thickets for things like rattle handles and other sacred crafting.

Devil's club is protective. We don't need intuition or a spiritual lens to grasp the protective quality of devil's club. Simply look at those spines that cover the whole body. This plant practically exudes protection. And those spines are not to be messed with. A prick by a devil's club spine can cause a reactive dermatitis that is unpleasant and takes time to heal, not to mention a potential staph infection. This plant teaches us how to clearly, undeniably, and unapologetically set a boundary that says, "NO!" when the answer is no. This medicine may help a person in need of a deeper sense of safety due to lingering effects of traumas or challenges in the past. Devil's club helps folks who tend to become overwhelmed or flooded by the energies of their external environments and provides spiritual protection from negative or unwanted influences of all kinds. In a plant spirit sit during an herb class, devil's club shared with a student, "I teach you that you can admire something, but you must respect it."

Devil's club teaches empowerment. The stalks of devil's club stand nearly perfectly upright. They stand tall and proud, unapologetically declaring to the world, "Here I am!" Their body's growth habit is very unique compared to the other plants with whom devil's club shares the forests and in this there is a medicine of authenticity, authentic expression, and empowerment the plant reflects to us. Devil's club teaches us to "grow a spine," to stand in our own truth, and to be the authentic expression of ourselves. Devil's club especially helps people who are struggling to embody their personal power in the face of past traumas, hard relationships, toxic surroundings, etc. Devil's club helps us to stand up and say, "I am here!" to take up and claim the space allotted for us.

Devil's club teaches humility. Devil's club holds the medicine of empowerment yet also of humility. After doing a plant spirit sit with devil's club, a student described the energy as "stately, subdued, confident, doesn't have to prove itself." We see this reflected in the fact that for half the year, during fall and winter, the plant is almost invisible to the naked eye in the forest. Unless we know where to look and find the brown stalks disappearing into the forest's veil, we may not notice the devil's club is even there.

Devil's club helps us rise above the chaos. Another of the unique attributes of devil's club is the tall and spiny bare stalks that are topped by a whorl of huge maple-like leaves. These leaves almost seem to make their own sub-canopy layer of the forest. Devil's club can help us to see above the turmoil of the moment, the day, the generation, and the epoch. The plant helps us connect to higher wisdom, the higher perspective. One student received the impression from devil's club that "the leaves look like hands from above, providing a shawl of protection."

Devil's club connects to higher wisdom. A friend lost her husband in a tragic and fatal accident. At the time of death, both husband and wife were committed spirit workers who carried a lot of medicine for the community. This commitment to spirit work did not change with death as evidenced by the following dream my friend received a few nights after her husband's passing. Her journal entry from the morning of the dream reads, "[He] was in my dream. He told me he is using lots of devil's club there, which is funny because I didn't think you need salves in the spirit world. But maybe you do. It makes me think maybe he was using it in different forms as a spiritual medicine. But I really thought I saw him smearing the salve on people who needed it. Ministering like an angel with the anointing salve."

This beautiful man's death shook many in the community down to their core, but his soul's commitment to helping the people did not perish alongside his physical body. On the other side, his spirit was working with devil's club, a plant who had very much been his ally when alive, to heal and protect the hearts of the people. Perhaps he and devil's club were encouraging loved ones left behind to connect to higher wisdom and see the bigger picture at play surrounding his own death.

Tincture — As mentioned, I don't recommend using devil's club as a full-strength tincture. Rather, I recommend taking the tincture in drop dose form. Add to blends for integrating personal power, boundaries, protection, and the like.

Infused oil/salve — Traditionally, this plant was painted onto the skin of ceremonial dancers in Native American cultures that grow where the plant grows. To emulate this spirit medicine, infuse a bit of the root bark into olive oil and then turn it into a salve, anointing the body with this salve for help with integrating the spiritual qualities.

Save sticks for ceremonial use — After garbling and removing the root bark from devil's club, there is a wood-like stick left over that infuses a powerful spirit into other projects, creations, and medicine uses. Rattle handles, drumbeater handles, prayer sticks, and curtain rods are just a few of the ways this part of the devil's club can be worked with. The sticks can be placed around the home, on window sills, by doors, next to the bed, etc., to imbue the area with devil's club's protective, empowering qualities.

Herbal Formula: Empowered Tincture

This blend serves to awaken and integrate a deep sense of connection to self, personal power, protection, and authentic expression. In the chakra model, this blend helps open and strengthen the third chakra—our power center. Anyone working to integrate a more rooted sense of authentic selfhood might choose to work with this blend in drop doses to facilitate that embodiment.

Prepare a tincture with equal parts of the following herbs, fresh or dried.

Devil's club inner bark
St. John's wort leaf and flower
Red cedar leaf
Yarrow flower

Directions: Take drop doses of this blend many times daily when working to integrate the power of empowerment.

Other Formulas:
Trauma Salve page 209

HUCKLEBERRY
Vaccinium ssp.

Red Huckleberry

Body Parts: Berries and leaves

Note: The red huckleberry (*Vaccinium parvifolium*) is one of many *Vaccinium* species that grow in the forests of the Pacific Northwest, though *Vaccinium* species can be found growing throughout North America. The healing gifts shared here apply to all *Vaccinium* species. While the spiritual gifts came through conversations with the red huckleberry in particular, they may be applicable to the *Vaccinium* genus in general. Find a huckleberry or blueberry, and consult them on the matter.

Harvesting: For just the berries, fingers are all that's required. If leaves are desired as well, use snips or scissors to remove berry-laden branches, twigs and all, snipping at one of the branching nodes.

Garbling: The leaves and berries must be removed from the hardier stems. Use either hands, snips, or scissors to pluck the berries and leaves from the stems.

Huckleberry loves the eyes. The berries are loaded with antioxidant compounds that promote healthy circulation to the microcapillaries in the eyes. By promoting healthy circulation, the berries can help prevent and even reverse the incidence of various eye diseases. They boost overall vitality in tired, strained eyes.

Huckleberry loves the urinary tract. The berries and leaves of the huckleberries are a helpful aid to the urinary tract and kidneys. As an antimicrobial and diuretic, they help to reduce the inflammation and irritation in these tissues and promote healing. I wouldn't rely on this plant alone to treat a urinary tract infection, but I definitely include it in formula with other herbs for the purpose. Cranberry is a *Vaccinium* cousin of huckleberry. If prone to regular UTIs and cranberry helps, then huckleberry will likely also help as they have similar constituent profiles.

Huckleberry brings play to decay. Huckleberries are those small, bright green shrubs we see growing straight out of the stumps of old trees. This is quite unique to them. The whole *Vaccinium* genus is known for its ability and need to grow in acidic soils. In the wild, these plants literally grow in actively decaying wood from the forest's trees. These plants grow in decay! For such a vibrant, cheery, sweet, and delicious plant, this juxtaposition is almost striking. How could so much light and sweetness grow in active decay and death? This is a hint to huckleberry's deeper medicine.

Huckleberry lightens us up. Red huckleberry was one of the first plants to befriend me back in herb school at Bastyr University. It was the first quarter of school in our Introduction to Herbalism class and this was our first official foray into the herbalism of herb school. It was a big deal! We were given an assignment to "find our first plant ally." At that point in my life journey, my interspecies communication skills were hugely underdeveloped as was my self-confidence. I deeply struggled with self-doubt. *I would be able to talk to a plant?! Yeah right. That was only for special, gifted, REAL herbalists!* But lo and behold, while out strolling through the woods one day, this gorgeous red huckleberry bush pulled on my subtle sleeve and enfolded me into an energetic embrace. Sitting with this plant, not believing what was really happening, I did indeed receive messages and impressions. They floated into my mind and shifted my feeling state. *Wow! So this is how it works! But it was real!* The huckleberry was quite literally telling me to lighten up and not take it all so seriously. The path of herbalism and communicating with the plants should be fun and enjoyable. A childlike mind and a sense of wonder open the doors to these magical worlds. In essence, huckleberry taught me to *lighten up!* This medicine worked on me in many ways, opening the doorway to my ability to be in communion with the plants and teaching me that ever-important lesson of the wild walk: Lighten up. Receive the enchantment that is naturally here. Enjoy the ride.

When one feels like they've lost their sense of wonder, are taking things too seriously, or have become too encrusted with work, obligations, and expectations, huckleberry reflects that sense of childlike wonder and the ability to grow light, delicious, and beautiful on and amidst decay.

Nibble fresh — Of course, huckleberries can and should be grazed upon whenever they are ripe and delicious.

Tincture — Tincture the leaves and berries together fresh to help support the circulation and urinary systems.

Dry for infusions — The leaves can be dried and taken as infusions for the same support described above.

Herbal Formula: Urinary Soother Drops

Work with this formula during symptoms of urinary tract infection (UTI) or discomfort. Note: Herbs often work quite well when taken for UTIs. However, the choice comes with a level of personal accountability. The herbs should be taken regularly in higher doses (see dosing section for acute situations on page 259) and it is imperative to monitor the kidneys to determine if the infection is spreading. If the kidneys start to hurt, get to the doctor right away.

Prepare the following fresh or dried plants as a tincture.

50% uva ursi leaf
20% huckleberry or other *Vaccinium*
10% juniper berry
10% Oregon grape root
10% yarrow flower

Directions: Consider taking 1 to 2 droppersful 4 to 6x daily during an infection. For folks prone to UTIs, consider taking 2 droppersful 3x daily for a few days after engaging in a triggering activity, such as sex, travel, eating sugary foods, or whatever it might be.

Fall

HAWTHORN
Crataegus spp.

Body Parts: Berries

Other Parts at Other Times:
* Early summer — Harvest flowers and leaves.

Harvesting: When the magical hawthorn trees are drooping with the weight of their delicious red berries, it's time to head out and harvest. Use fingers to pluck off the clusters of berries, leaving all sticks and branches on the tree.

Hawthorn is heart medicine. Hawthorn berries very well may be the best natural substance on Earth for the human heart. The berries are full of anti-inflammatory flavonoids that decrease oxidation and inflammation in the cardiovascular system. They promote healthy blood pressure, cholesterol levels, overall circulation, and protection of the heart itself. They improve cardiac circulation, helping increase the amount of oxygen and blood flow to the heart. They help the heart do its job better, lightening the load. They can help stabilize an irregular heartbeat, decrease feelings of angina, and perhaps help decrease the incidence of heart attack.

Hawthorn opens the airways. In Chinese medicine, the lungs and heart are on the same channel. This is why, as many of us now know, grief often resides in the lungs. Thanks to the work of Dr. Deborah Frances, we've learned that hawthorn is a powerful ally for dealing with asthma and chronic lung congestion.[1] The plant helps open up the heart/lung channel leading to bronchodilation and has antihistamine properties. Hawthorn is definitely a plant worth considering for those plagued by asthma or lung congestion.

Hawthorn soothes anxiety that lives in the heart. Hawthorn is a relaxing nervine with an affinity for the heart. It relieves nervous system tension, anxiety, depression, panic, or any emotional-psycho-spiritual pattern causing constriction in the heart, chest, and throat areas. Hawthorn relaxes and soothes the nerves around these areas of the body, leading to a decrease in the physical experience of tightness and stress in the chest.

Hawthorn opens the heart. In any situation in which a blocking, stuckness, or toughness is plaguing the heart, hawthorn helps to open the heart channel so that life-giving energy can flow. Life-giving energy does not mean "feel-good energy." Life-giving energy means *real energy*—life energy! Oftentimes it is a backlog of grief, anger, or resentments that causes stagnation in the heart, leading to unpleasant physical sensations. Hawthorn reliably opens the heart channel so that the grief can flow, the anger and resentments can break up and life, and perhaps even the flowering of life, can return. When grief, loss, heartbreak, and heartache are moving through the heart in heavy amounts, hawthorn can sit with that grief and help us not get stuck in it.

Hawthorn teaches abundance and generosity. Simply gaze upon a berry-laden hawthorn tree and vibrations of abundance permeate the atmosphere. Hawthorn is so giving, so plentiful, so generous! Hawthorn gives and gives and teaches us that we too can and should be generous when in our full flower. We too are the abundant flowering of Creation.

Hawthorn teaches about boundaries. When gazing upon this abundant, berry-laden and beautiful nature of hawthorn, you would never assume that hidden right within those blankets of berries are gnarly two-inch-long spines that are like tiny daggers. In this, hawthorn teaches us how to have healthy boundaries. Boundaries are not walls that harden us to life and to love and dim our beauty. Far from it. We radiate our beauty, love, and authenticity, opening our hearts generously to love and to life. But we don't lose ourselves in this open-hearted state. Our boundaries are still available when our beauty and generosity aren't being righteously protected, respected, or cherished by others.

Hawthorn connects us to the Fairy realm. In the Celtic tradition, hawthorn is considered to be nothing less than a sacred and holy being. Still today in Ireland, it is considered very bad luck to cut down a hawthorn tree. Fairies are the beings who live in the Celtic Otherworld, the realm just on the other side of the veil from our own. When a hawthorn tree is cut down without proper respect, the Fairies are known to exact their revenge by ruining any plans or projects one had for the area where the hawthorn tree was cut. Hawthorn is sacred to the time of Beltane or May Day, when that veil between the Fairy realm and our human realm becomes quite thin. The hawthorn tree is the doorway to the realm of Fairy, where it proves to be a most valuable ally when working to integrate one's own relationship to the Fairies or Celtic ancestry.

Hawthorn is an ally for addiction. This teaching from hawthorn came to me in a dream in which hawthorn simply whispered into my dream ear, "I help people moving through addiction." As I've sat with this dream, I've come to understand that by soothing the heart channel, essential when one is taking the heroic steps of removing an addictive substance, hawthorn eases the process just a bit. Hawthorn soothes the heart during the transition time, keeping the heart open and flowing so the necessary feelings and wounds can be processed and helping a person stay connected to their heart's deep intention. Hawthorn also helps with boundary setting within oneself.

Tincture — These days, hawthorn tincture ends up in at least half of the formulas I create. This plant and I are deep soul friends and I love sharing with others the healing blessings born from our relationship. Also, this is a time on Earth of much unmetabolized grief, heartache, and heartbreak, all of which play a very real role in our physical and spiritual healing. Hawthorn catalyzes the heart, bringing its healing energy into the process. Love heals. Hawthorn helps.

Note: When fresh, hawthorn berries are loaded with pectin—they are close cousins of apples—and when tinctured fresh, a floating glob of gel arrives in the jar. Don't freak out. That gel-like blob is supposed to be there! It's the pectin. After straining, the pectin will integrate more evenly into the solution of the tincture. This phenomenon doesn't occur when the berries are already dried.

Syrup — The pectin content of hawthorn berries makes them a wonderful candidate for medicinal syrups. Especially for those who don't like tinctures.

Dry for infusions — Fresh hawthorn berries become like little stone pebbles when dried. It helps to grind them with a mortar and pestle to open the cell walls to the hot water. They are a wonderful addition to tea blends.

Herbal Formula: Heart Hug Tincture

This trio of heart-supportive herbs soothes and hugs the heart anytime it could use a little extra lovin'. This blend will open the heart channel so the life-giving energies of grief and relief can flow. It also helps us feel soothed and lightened in the process.

Prepare a tincture of equal parts of the following fresh or dried herbs.

Hawthorn berry
Wild rose petal
Motherwort herb

Directions: Take a few drops of this goddess trio as often as you need it throughout the day.

Other Formulas:
Tincture for the Grouchies page 123

Fall

ROSE HIPS
Rosa spp.

Note: All species of roses make hips. All hips are edible and medicinal. The hips of the wild roses are smaller than many of the cultivated varieties. Thus, the wild species can be more difficult and laborious to harvest and garble.

Body Parts: Hips

Other Parts at Other Times:
* Spring — Snip the leaves.
* Summer— Snip the flowers.

Harvesting: The time after the first frost of the year and before the hard freeze of winter is ideal and brings out the best of the hips' juicy nature. Use snips, scissors, or hands to pluck the hips off and into the harvest basket.

Garbling: Inside the fleshy hips are seeds surrounded by a mass of tiny hairs, which need to be removed before ingesting or processing. Both the seeds and the hairs are irritating to tissues in the mouth, throat, and digestive tract. While they're still fresh, use a paring knife to slice the hips in half. Then use the tip of a dull butter knife to gently scrape out all the innards of the hips. These hollowed-out hip halves can be dried using any drying method. Once dry, place the hips in a wire mesh colander and give them a good shake. This will pull off any remaining hairs or seeds. Voila! Edible hips of the goddess.

Rose hips house Vitamin C. Rose hips are loaded with vitamin C and other antioxidant compounds. They are fabulously supportive and protective of the heart, blood vessels, and entire cardiovascular system. They generally serve as a body-wide antioxidant and can be thought of as a superfood. They're a great tonic and boost to the immune system to build immunity and to fight active infection. Add rose hips to any immune teas to boost vitamin C content and improve flavor.

Dry for infusions — Tea of dried rose hips is light, sweetish, and truly delightful. The hips combine beautifully with other less tasty and more punchy herbs. Add rose hips to formulas for immune health, cardiovascular health, and general antioxidant support.

Syrup — The hips combine beautifully in a sugar or honey syrup as an immune or cardiovascular tonic or just a heart-opening sweet delight.

Herbal Formula: Quick Rose Hip Jam

This is one of the easiest recipes there is! Simply cover the dried hips with apple juice in a jar and let sit overnight. The next day, it will have congealed into a jam. Eat this delicious jam by the spoonful, add to a cup of hot water, or spread over toast. It's a beautiful heart-opening treat.

BLUE ELDERBERRY
Sambucus cerulea

Body Parts: Berries

Other Parts at Other Times:
* Early summer — Harvest flowers before they are pollinated.

Safety: There are multiple species of elder, or *Sambucus*, that grow wild. In my area, the red elder (*Sambucus racemosa*) is the native species found abundantly. These red elders have bright red berries that are not suitable for human consumption as they are considered too high in the constituent cyanide. Only work with dried berries as cyanide is present in the fresh seeds of all species of elder and can cause nausea or dizziness when the berries are eaten fresh. The blue elder (*Sambucus cerulea*) grows natively in some parts of North America, is wonderfully medicinal, and is safe for consumption. This blue elder, as well as the European black elder (*Sambucus nigra*), readily and easily establish themselves in the garden.

Harvesting: Use loppers to reach up and snip off the whole panicle of gorgeous cloudy blue berries, floral stems and all. It's easiest to dry the berries when still attached to the panicle.

Garbling: For tincturing, it's appropriate to work with the fresh berries. Use snips, scissors, or fingers to remove all the berries from the floral stems. Note that berries will stain the fingers. For syrups and teas, the berries need to be dried out. To do so, lay the bundles of berries out until they are dry or put them under the oven light. Once dried, the berries will easily fall off the floral stems and are ready for storage.

Elder fights viruses. Elderberries are directly antiviral against influenza, rhinovirus, and the herpes virus. They work to prevent viral infection and to decrease the duration and severity of symptoms when there is an active infection.

Elder provides seasonal fortification. Elder protects and supports the body through colds, flus, and other seasonal respiratory and immune challenges. These berries are taken throughout the cold and flu season to build up innate immunity and in higher doses to treat acute viral infections.

Elder is safe. Safe for kids, safe for elders, safe to take long-term, safe for the whole family—a staple in the medicine cabinet of all families.

Elder guards thresholds. Sacred to the time of Samhain/Halloween, in the Celtic tradition, elder is said to guard the Samhain threshold between this world and the Otherworld. The Otherworld is the land of the ancestors, the fairies, and the spirits. We see elder trees serving this purpose out in the woodlands. Elder will often grow at edges, gateways, passageways, thresholds, and areas where the land switches from one "realm" to another. In this, it might be said that elder lives in the veil—the place in between. Said another way, elder guards the veil. Master herbalist Donald Yance says, "Elder is the tree of healing, rebirth, and resurrection."[2] Just as elder guards the darker times of the year, elder also holds threshold space for rebirth. Perhaps this is why elder is so powerful at times of seasonal sickness, which can be seen as a cleanse or reset. Elder helps to smooth out the little death/letting go/rebirth we endure each time our bodies catch a cold or flu.

Elder is the gateway herb. I call elder a gateway herb because I have converted many skeptics to the woo of herbal medicine by introducing them to elderberry syrup. The syrup debunks many common misbeliefs about herbalism and thus serves as a "gateway" to deepening relations with the plants.

How does elder convert the skeptics? First, everyone gets sick sometimes and elder really *works* to fight off seasonal infections. Second, the syrup tastes great and good taste always increases compliance. Third, making our own syrup is empowering! It's easy to make on one's own and doing so often demystifies the belief that herbalism is too hard or too out of reach. I have given dried elderberries along with a make-your-own-syrup recipe to countless nonbelievers and newbies. I'm happy to report there have been many converts, thanks to elder the threshold tender, for rebirthing people into the possibility and power of herbalism.

Elders help us sit with death. Elder is a powerful plant to work with during transitions of all kinds, including letting go, initiations, and deaths as this plant knows these thresholds and between spaces very well. Two instances brought this teaching home to me.

First, elder visited me in a night dream. At the time that the dream came, my heart was broken by the death of a young child in my community. The death rattled me and many around me deeply. In the dream, a midwife spirit—herself a tender of the threshold—visited me and said, "The mother of that lost child, and the whole community, need elder to help them *sit with death*." I woke up with gratitude for the visitation and teaching and upon awakening went and sat with an elder tree in the forest, praying that she help us all move through this incredible initiation and loss.

On another occasion, I was teaching a plant spirit medicine class on connecting with elder. The class was offered right around the Samhain threshold time. Only one woman showed up to the class, an unusual occurrence for my herb classes. But I trusted Spirit's hand in the process. Come to discover, elder had been stalking this woman with a series of remarkable synchronicities over the previous weeks. Clearly the plant was calling to her. As the night wore on, in the intimacy of such a tiny group, she shared that she was in a major initiation process of supporting her longtime husband, who was in the process of a slow death from a neurodegenerative disease. She was quite literally holding the threshold for him. It was no wonder elder was reaching out trying to help and had called her to attend class on that stormy fall night.

Elders are elders. The name is the medicine. Elder is an elder of the forest, holding the sage or crone-like vibration of Creation. For this reason, it's considered bad luck to cut down an elder tree and good luck to plant one near the home. Sitting at the feet of this wise elder can connect us to ancestral wisdom, to the wise one within, and to grow wisdom in our beings. As my three-year-old daughter, never having heard this teaching before, spontaneously sang in front of an elder tree near Samhain, "Mom! The ancestors are here!" She then proceeded to do a little jig, waving the feather she was holding toward the tree before dancing off toward something else exciting. Children are remarkable crones if we can slow down and listen deep enough to catch their pearls of wisdom.

Dry for syrup and infusions — The majority of harvested berries will likely be dried and made into syrups. The berries do make a lovely infusion and mix well with other immune herbs.

Tincture — The tincture is nice to have on hand to mix into tincture blends for colds, flus, and viral challenges. Tincture can be prepared from fresh or dried berries, though fresh berries are best in tincture as it is a safe way to utilize the fresh potency and vitality

Herbal Formula: Elderberry Syrup

Follow the recipe on page 240 for preparing elderberry syrup. Consider keeping a batch of this syrup whipped up and ready in the fridge during the cold and flu months of the year. Try adding a stick of cinnamon to the simmering elderberry syrup for more flavor and medicinal punch.

Dosing for prevention — Throughout the entire cold and flu season, consider taking 1 tablespoon daily of the syrup (1 teaspoon for kids) to keep those immune-boosting antiviral compounds circulating through the body. Elderberry syrup can also be added to smoothies, mixed in yogurts, or poured on pancakes or ice cream!

Dosing for treatment — At first sign of sickness or when exposed to people who might be sick, increase the dosing to 1 tablespoon for grownups (1 teaspoon for kids) every couple of hours. Continue at this higher dosing until symptoms improve. They will likely improve faster than they would without the elderberry syrup!

Going Deeper into Fall

In the Wild
Burdock seed — A reliable diuretic and kidney tonic.
* Tincture

Nettle seed — Invigorating and energizing, tonifying to the kidneys, and adaptogenic.
* Dry for eating & infusions
* Tincture

Wild carrot seed — Growing in disturbed areas, these seeds are a reliable pelvic decongestant, emmenagogue, and ally of female reproductive health. Don't consume when pregnant.
* Dry for chewing on & infusions
* Tincture

Safety Warning: *This plant looks very similar to its lethal cousin Poison Hemlock. Follow the Safety Rule on Page 60*

In the Garden
Fennel seed — Fennel grows abundantly and easily with little maintenance. Harvest the aromatic seeds for a fabulous carminative, or gas and bloating remedy.
* Dry for chewing on & infusions
* Tincture
* Glycerite

Chapter 7:
Winter

Winter Spirit Walk

It's undeniable now that winter has arrived. When we head outside to greet the Father Sun, our bones are chilled, there is frost on the ground, and we can feel it in the air: Nature is sleeping. We look around at our plant friends and teachers and see that the threshold time of fall has done its job. The aboveground parts of the plants' bodies have retreated back to be reintegrated into the web of life and the soil matrix. All that's left aboveground are the bones of the plants. The dried-out dormant stalks and trunks are holding the vision of life reemerging in spring, just as our ancestors hold that vision for us, dreaming our reemergence and continued life.

The grief from the fall threshold has been washed away and now we feel a stillness, an emptiness even. A space that is being held empty in order to hopefully be caught by the dreams the Mother Earth sends into our own dreamspaces.

"Come," the forest beckons us. This time, the forest feels indistinguishable from the voice of our ancestors. The voice feels ancient. The voice feels like bones, the bones of the Earth. "Come and sit, my children, and listen."

We bundle up and set out to walk with winter and the plants. Looking around, it's almost hard to remember which plants grew where. The land is either empty of growth or has indistinguishable plant bones growing on it. We have to dig deep to remember the life of spring and summer. We think of our ancestors, the long lineage of people from whom we descend, who are now just memories or echoes from the past. We know that in their time, their lives were big and important and beautiful and flowering and we are reminded that death comes to all of life.

Moving deeper into the forest, reflecting so deeply on our ancestors and the Dream of the Earth, we didn't realize we'd arrived at the sacred grove of red cedar trees. And lo and behold, they are still green! Here they are, these ancient evergreen ones keeping the Dream of the Earth, the promise of life and growth, alive for all of us. For all of life.

Taking in the scent of the cedars, we breathe their medicine deeply into our hearts, letting this encounter with these wise ones awaken our own evergreen nature. We feel the part of us that knows that the spark of life still lives within during this time of great quiet, great stillness, great hibernation, and great dreaming.

Reflecting on this evergreen nature within and without, we are invited by the cedar trees to drift down into the web of life underground. As our sacred imagination is drawn down into the web, we encounter the mycelium and all the little roots and rootlets that interweave to create this web of life. We're reminded that life is still beaming and teaming under here and that this is the same with our beloved medicinal plants. If the ground is squishy enough to be dug and worked, then those medicinal roots can be dug up. We decide that this will be our task later today: to go root digging before the hard freeze hits for the rest of winter.

"Come, children," beckons an ancient cedar. "Lean your bodies against mine and let me help you connect into the Dream of the Earth. Perhaps you will be lucky enough to be caught by a dream that you can give birth to come spring. Let me teach you about belonging to this land, of what it means to live a life worthy of being an honored ancestor when your time is past." Snuggling into our coats, scarves, and hats, we lean back into the loving strength of this wise ancient grandparent.

Winter Spirit Medicine

Winter is for dreaming. During winter, our energies are called within. The darker and colder conditions reflect the movement of life from a more outward focus to an inward gaze. It's the time to focus on the inner life, the energies moving within and the energies that are gestating. Winter is the time for dreaming, in the expanded sense of the word "dreaming." We sleep more, often more deeply, so it is the time when our dreams might be more readily accessible. And it's also time for the daytime dreaming, the conversations with the deep heart of nature, of the Dream of the Earth, about what it is that she is asking of us in the growing times to come. Winter is a time for reflection, for journeying, for journaling, for deep inquiry, and for deep conversations with all of life.

Winter is for assimilating and gestating. Winter is the time of year when our outward expressions have fallen away. For the plants, this is literally true—their bodies have died. We too have died ourselves, with all old masks having been stripped. Winter is the time to drop into the depth and truth of who we are underneath it all. Underneath all our identities, our masks, our roles: Who are we? What matters to us? Why are we here? What do we serve? Why? What are we creating on behalf of our nature-given lives? These questions we ponder as we assimilate and integrate all that we have done and been in the preceding growing times. We gestate who and how we will emerge when spring finally does arrive.

Winter Spirit Medicine Reflections

Find a spot in nature that feels blessed and sacred to you. You might be called to a place with evergreen plants or perhaps it is a place where only the plant bones remain.

A grove of red cedars or other coniferous trees is usually a place where the sacred in nature can be strongly sensed during winter as the spark of life is still present in their evergreen bodies. Plug yourself into the web of life, asking the web, the land, and the plants in their winter clothes to help you answer the following questions.

* What would the Dream of the Earth like me to reflect upon in the remaining winter?

* What dreams am I gestating this winter?

* What can I do that will please my ancestors?

* How can I better cultivate myself into an ancestor worth claiming?

* How can I serve the plants when it is their (our) growing time again, come spring?

* How can I give back to feed all of life?

Winter Herbalism

In winter we have crossed the fall threshold. Except for the evergreens, the plant bodies have died back and retreated to life underground. In winter most plants are storing all of their energy, and thus their medicinal constituents, in the roots of their bodies. And so this is the time we think about harvesting roots. Early winter is the time for root digging, right around the turn from fall. We want to root dig when the ground still hasn't gone into hard freeze and the soil can still be turned. Once the hard freeze hits, then it is truly time for the rest and rejuvenation of winter.

RED CEDAR
Thuja plicata

Body Parts: Leaves, also known as fronds

Harvesting: Red cedar leaves may be harvested at any point throughout the year, the best time being when they find us! Whenever we might be so blessed as to find fallen branches, give the leaves a smell and a taste. If they taste and smell potent, aromatic, and cedar-like, then their medicine is strong. Red cedar is included here in winter as the solstice is a beautiful time to drop into this plant's deep medicine. Use snips, scissors, or fingers to tear the fronds or leaves from the branches.

Safety: Contraindicated in pregnancy or breastfeeding and in the case of kidney disease or weakness. Not appropriate for long-term use. Red cedar is a low-dose plant, meaning it should not be ingested as a simple at regular doses. Instead, red cedar can be added to formulas mixed with other more benign herbs or taken at drop dosing for spiritual support. If we remain under 10 drops of tincture each day, we will keep a good distance away from approaching a toxic dose.

Red cedar clears the lungs. Trees are the lungs of the Earth and coniferous/evergreen trees generally have an opening and clearing effect on the respiratory system. They help our bodies breathe better. Red cedar leaves are loaded with essential oil constituents that serve to decongest, decrease mucus, soothe the cough impulse, and fight infections in the respiratory tract.

Red cedar fights fungus. Red cedar leaves are uniquely antifungal, providing excellent support for fungal skin infections, such as athlete's foot, nail fungus, and ringworm. Internally cedar helps to address yeast imbalances, especially in the urinary tract and vagina.

Red cedar is the Tree of Life. Red cedar is honored as the Tree of Life in the coastal regions where it is native. Jim Pojar and Andy MacKinnon state in their book *Plants of the Pacific Northwest Coast,* "Red Cedar is the cornerstone of Northwest Coast Indian culture. The large-scale use of its wood and bark delineates the cultural boundary of Northwest Coast peoples within its range."[2] Pre-colonization, this tree quite literally gave, supported, and nurtured the life of the people. House planks, totem poles, baskets, clothing, hats, dishware, tools, canoes, food, medicine—all of these were made from the body of the red cedar and it remains a cornerstone in Coast

Salish culture today. For those of us who live in red cedar territory, these trees can teach us about what it means to be the Tree of Life. What does it mean to feed life? What does it mean to nurture, sustain, and suckle life? What does it mean to be a nurse log? What does it mean to be the grandparents of an entire ecosystem? Sit at the feet of a red cedar and ponder these questions. As the Tree of Life in its bioregion, red cedar opens these life-sustaining pathways within our own beings while nurturing our belonging to the land we call home.

Red cedar reweaves us into the Dream of the Earth. As the Tree of Life, red cedar serves as a guide and guardian for reconnection with the Dream of the Earth. Sit in a red cedar grove or connect with red cedar medicine, asking this wise grandparent to introduce you to the web of life and to help reweave membership within it. What does it mean to be a member of the web of life? What is the dream of the land in this region? What does the land want for itself? What does Mother Earth want for this piece of land? What can we do to serve that dream on behalf of all of life? Red cedar guides us into these ponderings and heals the places within us that might feel we don't deserve to ask these questions.

Red cedar is protective. Simply sitting with our backs leaned up against a red cedar tree will introduce us to its strong protection medicine. Red cedar feeds the energies of ancient support, deep grounding, and unconditional belonging, connecting us to the core of our essential nature so that we become protected from any negativities.

Red cedar supports relationships. Years ago I was given a dream. In this dream I am walking in a forest and my mind's eye merges with an old red cedar tree. This tree is standing just opposite and facing another old red cedar tree. It is clear these two trees are mated. Red cedar tells me, "This is how you safely enter into relationship with another. Both parties must be deeply rooted, grounded, and connected into the truth of their own beings. From this grounded sense of self, it is safe to open to intimacy with another rooted being." As I've sat with this, I've come to understand that red cedar helps us to integrate opposites. This is true on all levels. Red cedar helps us integrate the opposites within our own beings in the Sacred Marriage, within our relationships—regardless of gender identities or sexual preferences—and indeed within the collective as a whole.

Tincture — Tincture the fresh leaves and add to formulas that support respiratory, vaginal, and urinary health. Work with the tincture in drop dose form as spirit medicine.

Infused oil — Red cedar-infused oil is excellent for anointing the body for protection or for integrating spirit medicine. Include in salves for skin infections, fungal support, and as a general anti-inflammatory.

Dry for infusions — A few of the dried leaves are a delicious addition to tea blends for respiratory support.

Dry for smudge — Red cedar leaves can be burned for smudging purposes, either loose or wrapped as a smudge wand.

Cedar Smudge

People around the world have traditions of lighting aromatic herbs aflame to ignite and utilize the spiritual properties of the plants. "Smudging" is the term used in Native American spirituality while Celtic practitioners use the word "saining." The terms "incense" and "smoke bath" are other names given to this simple but powerful ceremony. Plants that make for good smudging are high in essential oils, so they have a pleasant aroma when burning, and burn easily and well.

Working with plants that grow where we grow takes the load off of the more popular smudging herbs, such as white sage, a plant who is sadly growing more endangered each year. Red cedar is the smudge herb of the Pacific Northwest bioregion. It grows abundantly, burns well, smells divine, and is highly cleansing and protective. If red cedar doesn't grow in your area, with a bit of research you will no doubt find a smudge plant that does.

Folks who've never smudged before can be intimidated by the process, thinking it requires a fancy complicated procedure. Far from it! We can all easily learn how to work with healing plants to spiritually cleanse ourselves. A regular smudging practice really makes a difference in maintaining our "energy hygiene" in this world. The cost is free or at the very least inexpensive. It's easily accessible, powerful, and effective.

How to Smudge

First, connect from the heart with the spirit of the plant. Send gratitude for the plant's medicine and for its help in bringing cleansing and healing. Then bring fire to the plant and move the smoke around your body, making certain to smudge the bottoms of the feet and the top of the head. Sometimes we are called by an unknown impulse to linger on a particular body part. If that impulse arises, follow it. The plant is doing some extra medicine work in that specific area of the body and we'd be wise to let it happen. Our instincts inform us when that work is done and it's time to move on. The entire process usually takes less than two minutes and leaves us feeling refreshed, regrounded, and renewed.

The same procedure holds true if we are smudging a home, space, item, another person, or whatever we might be called to. We can't get it wrong. Our job is to let the plants do the work.

Herbal Formula: Fight the Fungus Salve

This highly antifungal blend is applied topically to fight athlete's foot, ringworm, toe and nail fungus, and general fungal skin infections. It's a combo of local Pacific Northwest herbs plus either red cedar essential oil (known as thuja oil) and/or tea tree essential oil.

Prepare an infused oil of equal parts of the following herbs.

Red cedar leaf
Calendula flower
Oregon grape root
Cottonwood bud

After removal from heat, add 30 drops combined total of thuja (red cedar) and/or tea tree essential oil to each cup of herbal oil. Then add beeswax to turn into a salve.

Other Formulas:
Spirit Reset Bath page 138
Empowered Tincture page 155

OREGON GRAPE
Mahonia nervosa

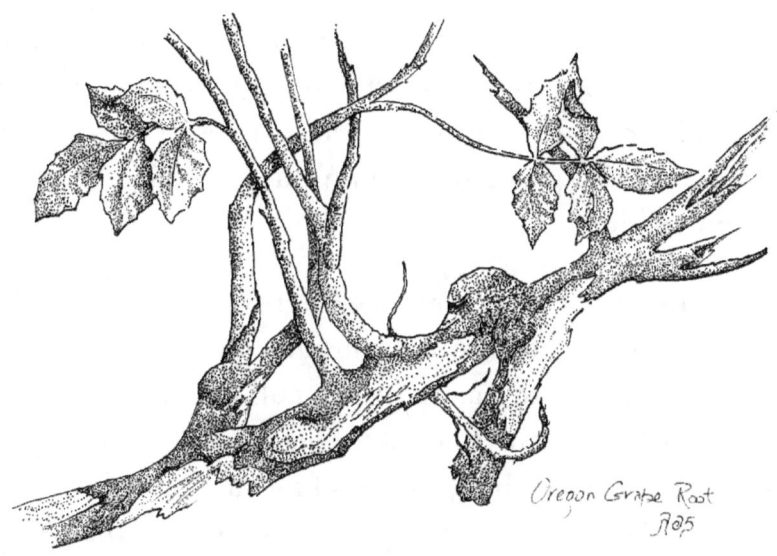

Body Parts: Roots

Sustainability Note: United Plant Savers (UPS) is a fabulous organization dedicated to the preservation of native North American medicinal plants. UPS lists Oregon grape on its "at-risk" list, meaning that wild harvesting should be limited and monitored.[1] Though you wouldn't know it when out in the many forested areas where the Oregon grape is abundant and plentiful, this plant's native habitat is indeed threatened. Oregon grape is a forest dweller, which means that in order for its populations to thrive it needs forests. Forests are unfortunately a rapidly dwindling ecosystem. Even though Oregon grape grows plentifully in some places, it's important that we see the bigger picture and harvest sparingly, allowing this plant to awaken the stewardship and protective aspects of our herbal nature. Though considered at-risk, I've opted to include Oregon grape for a few compelling reasons. First, Oregon grape is a most excellent antimicrobial. Because of its powerful antimicrobial nature, it's easy to use sparingly as we only need a little bit on hand to administer in the rare cases we need it. Second, with just a wee bit of know-how, Oregon grape can be easily repropagated and/or integrated into the garden or landscape, thereby diminishing our impacts on the wild populations.

Harvesting: Oregon grape likes to grow in thickets, often seen covering whole forest hillsides in beautiful dense blankets. Using both hands, gently pull on the plants until one is found that seems to want to come loose. Then dig away the dirt by hand while gently jostling the plant free or by using a hori-hori, shovel, or digging fork to aid in the process of coaxing the rhizome out. Keep jostling and gently digging until either the rhizome breaks or the end of the root comes out.

Replanting: Leave a few inches of rhizome attached to the crown of the plant. Cut away the leaves and then replant this crown in the hole where it was dug out. Done properly, with the grace of nature, these crowns will regrow even with their roots removed.

Garbling: It's a good idea to garble these roots as soon as possible as they become very hard and nearly impossible to work with when dried. Use a knife to chop the roots into small pieces before drying or adding to a maceration.

Safety: Contraindicated during pregnancy. Not appropriate for long-term use.

Oregon Grape fights infections. The inner root bark of Oregon grape is a beautiful and brilliant bright yellow, loaded with a special plant constituent called berberine. Berberine is also present in the infamous, highly overharvested, and now nearly extinct plant goldenseal. It's preferable to work with Oregon grape to lighten the load on goldenseal. Let us hope and pray that the same fate doesn't befall this plant as befell its cousin. Berberine is one of the strongest antibiotic constituents in the plant kingdom and can be called upon for all varieties of infectious experiences. Proven to be helpful for many bacterial and parasitic infections, Oregon grape is especially useful in the gut for digestive infections and disturbances of all kinds, such as infectious diarrhea, giardia, candida, and the like. Oregon grape also brings antimicrobial aid to infections in the vagina, respiratory tract, and sinuses.

Oregon grape loves the liver. Oregon grape is bitter and bitters generally have a detoxifying effect on the body. This plant stimulates digestive secretions, liver detoxification, gallbladder secretions, kidney filtration, and lymphatic circulation. Oregon grape can be helpful for all kinds of stagnations, such as inflammatory skin conditions, arthritic joints, and the like.

Oregon grape is protective. The holly-like evergreen leaves of Oregon grape are quite unique. They're poky, but not *too* poky. Oregon grape teaches us to set just the right amount of boundaries, have just the right amount of discernment, and apply just the right amount of protection to keep us safe when navigating the world. Oregon grape helps teach us the finesse of being authentic and wise in protecting our energy.

Oregon grape cleanses the spirit. Like all the bitter alterative plants, Oregon grape encourages the spirit to let go of old grievances, old resentments, and old ways of being. The liver-cleansing qualities of Oregon grape help us release pent-up or unprocessed anger. The root really helps us to "dig deep" into the core of ourselves to shine that out in the world in all situations.

Oregon grape is authentic. Oregon grape has a strong affinity for authenticity, helping to cleanse the spirit of outdated and unauthentic ways of being. That bright yellow color could be described as associated with the third chakra, the part of our energy governing our authentic expression and embodiment. Oregon grape is unapologetically wild, evergreen, boundaried, bright, and bold.

Tincture — Oregon grape is preferable in tincture form as the roots are strong-acting and strong-tasting. Add Oregon grape to most formulas to treat infection. This is not a plant to take every day long-term, but one to take when needed and stop when health is restored.

Dry for infusions — Save some dried root to whip into a quick tea for treating digestive distress or to make into a compress to help fight a topical infection.

Infuse in oil — Being so antimicrobial, Oregon grape is a wonderful herb to add to topical salves for fighting infection.

Herbal Formula: The Big Guns Herbal Antimicrobial Tincture

This formula is a general antimicrobial tincture for colds, flus, and respiratory challenges. It contains "the big guns," herbs loaded with antimicrobial and decongestant infection-fighting power.

Prepare the following fresh or dried herbs as a tincture.

3 parts lomatium
2 parts Oregon grape root
2 parts usnea
1 part yerba santa
½ part ginger root

Directions: Consider taking 2 droppersful as needed 3 to 7x daily

Other Formulas:
Urinary Soother Drops page 160
Fight the Fungus Salve page 188
Healthy Skin Drops page 198

DANDELION
Taraxacum officinale

Body Parts: Roots

Other Parts at Other Times:
* Spring — Pick fresh leaves when they first emerge.
* Summer — Snip off the flower heads in summer.

Harvesting: By the arrival of fall, the telltale yellow flowers of dandelion are no longer out, forcing us to rely on our leaf identification skills. Make absolutely certain the plant is indeed dandelion and not one of the many close relatives with similar-looking flowers and habitats. Dandelion leaves are pointier, smoother, and more heavily serrated than the lookalikes. Use scissors or snips to trim at the base of the leaves around the basal rosette.

Dandelion cleanses. Dandelion is a supreme cleansing tonic. The entire plant is cooling and cleansing to the body. The whole plant is very bitter and thus provides all the healing and cooling properties of bitters. Dandelion stimulates and supports the liver, strengthens and improves overall digestion, and decreases gas, bloating, and digestive stagnation. Bitters are to be taken before meals to improve digestion and decrease discomfort. Bitters also help to alkalize and cool, generally having a detoxifying and anti-inflammatory effect on the body. Just like the roots that grow into the Mother Earth, when taken internally dandelion roots work to deeply cleanse and restore the whole body system. Dandelion supports the liver and kidneys to do their detoxification work better and more efficiently, helps remove inflammation and toxic metabolites from the joints, lymph, and blood, and is very cleansing to the digestive system.

Dandelion flushes. Dandelion is a powerful kidney tonic and reliable diuretic. Taken as tea, the roots—and the entire plant in fact—help to flush and support the kidneys and can aid in the release of water retention, such as in the case of edema, premenstrual swelling, and high blood pressure.

Dandelion makes radiant skin. Dandelion's medicine works wonders toward promoting radiant skin. Call on this cleansing ally to rebalance skin health in the case of acne, eczema, psoriasis, dandruff, rashes, and any inflammatory skin condition. Dandelion cleanses from the inside out, promoting the body's other detoxification methods so that toxins aren't being expressed through the skin.

Dandelion enlightens. Dandelion's spirit is pure, fierce sunshine, helping those times when we may be stuck in darkness. Darkness might cloud the physical body, manifesting as stagnation, stuckness, or sluggishness; in the mental-emotional body as deep old anger, rage, bitterness, or resentment; or in the spirit body as stuck patterns of energetic darkness or cloudiness. In these instances of darkness and sluggishness, dandelion comes in with a zesty ferociousness, helping to restore our commitment to life and reigniting the zest for life. Dandelion helps to cleanse out the old, reconnects us to our own inner light, revitalizes, and "gets us back out there" to live our lives with gusto.

Dandelion alchemizes anger. Dandelion is a powerful teacher and *alchemizer* of excess anger and rage we might be holding onto or having a hard time processing and integrating. Dandelion's cooling zest activates the liver and gallbladder to restore these organs to their highest processing power of these fiery energies, helping us to move through and metabolize them.

Dandelion helps us dig deep. Dandelion awakens an understanding of the importance of digging deep within to break through into new ways of being. Loaded with minerals, these roots are able to pull up resources from deep within the Mother Earth, showing us how we too can become more deeply resourced and able to dive within. Dandelion helps us muster the resources needed to continue on, move forward, move through, evolve, and expand. Call upon dandelion when feeling stuck, stagnant, overwhelmed, or clouded by old resentments, old stories, old angers, frustrations, and the like.

Tincture — Work with dandelion tincture as a simple or in formulas to support healthy skin, a healthy liver, and healthy kidneys. The tincture is also great to take as a digestive bitter. Store in the kitchen and take a few drops on the tongue before meals to stimulate better digestion and decrease post-meal bloating.

Dry for infusions — Dandelion root, often paired with burdock, is a fabulous tonic for daily or regular use to promote gentle cleansing and deeply rooted health.

Cook fresh — Fresh dandelion roots can be roasted with other winter root veggies like carrots, parsnips, beets, burdock roots, potatoes, etc.

Herbal Formula: Healthy Skin Drops

This tincture blend is composed of all wild PNW plants. It can be taken to address all kinds of inflammatory skin conditions like acne, eczema, psoriasis, dandruff, rosacea, and other chronic rashes.

Combine the following fresh or dried herbs and process them into a tincture.

30% dandelion root
20% burdock root
20% chickweed aerial part
20% cleavers leaf and stem
10% Oregon grape root

Directions: Consider taking 1 to 2 droppersful 3x daily.

Other Formulas:
Love Your Lymph Tincture page 91

Winter

COTTONWOOD
Populus balsamifera

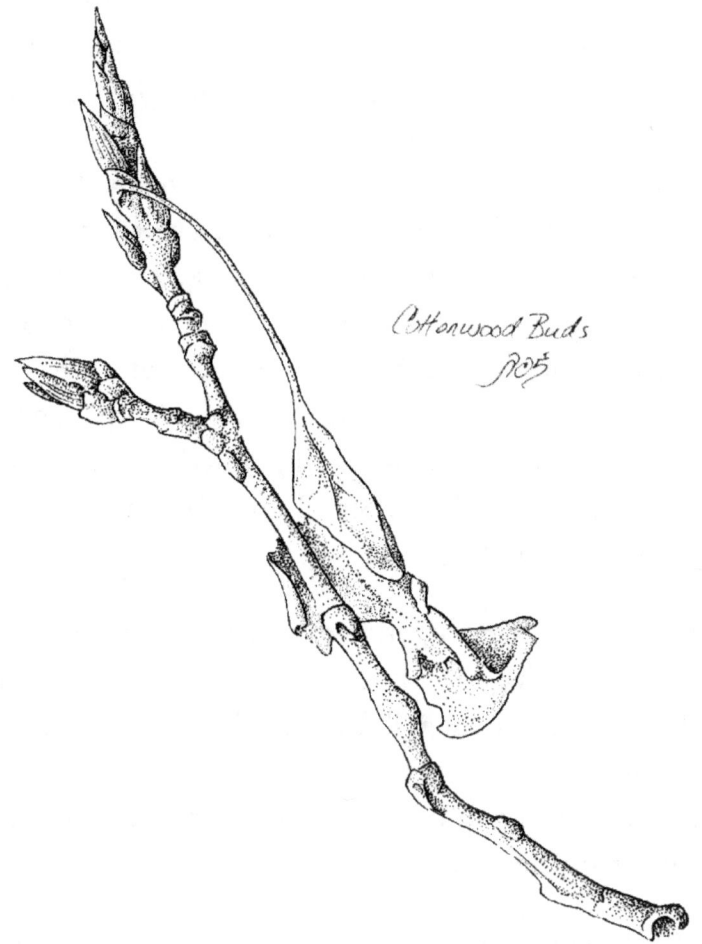

Body Parts: Buds

Naming: The common names cottonwood and poplar are used interchangeably as there are multiple subspecies of the *Populus balsamifera* tree. Balm of Gilead is another name for this plant, so highly prized in the ancient world that its healing prowess is mentioned by the name multiple times in the Christian Bible.

Harvesting: Around the turn of the New Year is a wonderful time to set out for these resinous wonders, though anytime from early winter through early spring when the leaves open will do. Following a windstorm is an ideal time to embark on a cottonwood mission as it's likely that many bud-laden branches have been blown from the trees. Every item or body part that the sticky buds touch will be stained with the resin, so choose tools with that in mind. Some people like to wear gloves. Others like to be bare-handed, knowing that their hands will be aromatic for a couple of days. Keep an eye out for the buds that are still closed and pointed. Avoid buds that feel squishy or molded out. Simply pop off the buds using bare or gloved fingers, leaving the sticks with the Earth.

Garbling: Fresh is far superior to dried buds, so it's best to get them macerating right away. As mentioned, any items or tools that the buds touch will be stained by the resin and will smell cottonwoody. A designated cottonwood crockpot is useful for processing into infused oil. Inexpensive used crock pots can usually be found at thrift stores.

Cottonwood makes an all-in-one healing salve. Cottonwood buds have a potent aromatic resin that makes an incredible topical healing salve, often called Balm of Gilead. When applied topically, the buds help to heal bumps, bruises, sprains, strains, injuries, and soft tissue trauma of all kinds. They also help improve circulation and detoxification, aiding in deeper arthritic inflammation, lymphatic swelling, and poor circulation. The resins are highly antimicrobial and antioxidant, making them incredible for wound care and skin care. The salve is truly an all-in-one healing ointment due to its versatility and effectiveness.

Cottonwood cleanses and protects the respiratory tract. Many herbally inclined people take propolis extract when fighting upper respiratory infections. But how many of us know that propolis is made from cottonwood buds? Propolis is a waxy resinous substance that bees make to line their hives. As an antioxidant and antiseptic, propolis prevents the hive from decay, providing a solid seal to protect the hive. The bees make their propolis from the resins gathered from the cottonwood buds. Cottonwood bud tincture can be taken internally in the same instances one would take propolis: to clear coughs and lung congestion, to soothe sore throats, to decrease mucus secretions in the upper and lower respiratory systems, and to protect from infection.

Cottonwood connects to the truth of the heart. Though each subspecies has slightly different leaf shapes, in general cottonwood's leaves are heart-shaped and in this there is a great medicine. Cottonwood teaches us to trust our heart's truth and knowing, even when that truth is in conflict with or doesn't make sense to the intellect. "The heart knows the way," the cottonwoods say. Sit with cottonwood when facing a difficult decision and in need of the wisdom and truth of the heart.

Cottonwood is a spirit dancer. Cottonwood is a spirit dancer, wind dancer, and whisperer of the voice of the holy and sacred forces of nature. Cottonwood leaves will dance, shake, and shimmer when no wind is blowing. In this they teach us the medicine of dancing one's authentic dance, even when circumstances are pulling us other ways. Never stop dancing and singing the truth of the heart.

Cottonwood can ride out the storm. This tree is highly associated with storms and wind. They are often planted as wind barriers on farmland and along highways because of the barrier effect they have on wind. The buds are best harvested after windstorms rush through. Cottonwood can teach us how to find the calm within the storm and stay deeply rooted in our truth while the storm plays itself out. It is a trusted ally for finding our way through and after the stormy times of life, for the leaves dance even when there is no wind.

Cottonwood opens the throat chakra. Cottonwood shared something of its medicine with me in a dream where I was helping a friend who was having a hard time standing in her authentic truth. A voice spoke to me, clearly and simply, "Cottonwood clears and empowers the throat channel. It helps when people experience anxiety, panic, and that closing-up feeling in the throat and heart." After this medicine was shared with my friend in the dream, her ears perked up and she started listening, her entire energy shifting and opening. I awoke, grateful to cottonwood for sharing this medicine and with the knowledge that healing was underway for the part of me that is reflected by my friend and perhaps for her as well.

Tincture — Make fresh tincture of the buds for respiratory challenges. Tincture can be taken in drop doses for spirit medicine support. Being so high in resins, the medicine of these buds doesn't extract well into water, so they are not frequently made into teas.

Infused oil — Oil prepared from cottonwood buds will find its way into many ointment recipes. Because the resins are so highly antioxidant and antiseptic, cottonwood oil has a longer shelf life than other herbal oils and is even utilized as a preservative in this regard.

Herbal Formula: Balm of Gilead

Due to its incredible versatility and efficacy, salve made from cottonwood buds should be a staple in all home medicine chests. To make this wondrous healing ointment, known as Balm of Gilead, start by making an infused oil of the buds utilizing the Crock Pot Method described on page 244. Add beeswax to the oil to turn it into an all-purpose healing salve.

Alternatively, the ointment can be made utilizing lard as the menstruum. Traditionally, the Coast Salish people of the Pacific Northwest infuse the buds in bear lard as an all-purpose healing salve. Inspired by this, I have worked with cottonwood buds in rendered pig lard, the closest substitute available for bear. The result is an incredibly powerful ointment. To work with lard as the menstruum, utilize the Crock Pot Method, making certain to strain the buds out while the lard is still warmed and in liquid form. Once the lard cools to room temperature it will solidify, negating the need to add beeswax for hardening.

Other Formulas:
Fight the Fungus Salve page 188
Trauma Salve page 209

COMFREY
Symphytum officinale

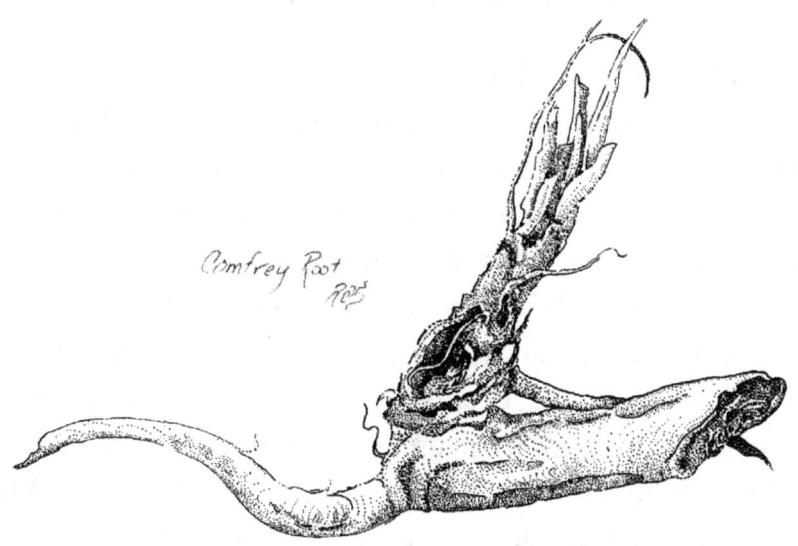

Body Parts: Roots

Harvesting: Though not originally native to North America, comfrey has naturalized into the wildscape of most disturbed areas in and around where people live and is a welcome and useful member of any home garden or farm. Warning: Comfrey grows abundantly, so plant with that in mind, knowing that the plant will establish well and spread. The roots can be dug up any time the plant starts to die back aboveground. Use a digging fork or shovel to dig the roots out from underground.

Garbling: As with all roots intended for medicine, comfrey must be processed and cut while still fresh. Once dry, they will turn as hard as rocks. Use pruning shears or loppers to dissect the root ball into smaller chunks as these are easier to work with. Fill a bucket with water and use a clean sponge to clean the dirt and debris from the roots. Once clean, slice the roots into 1- to 2-inch pieces before drying.

Safety: Comfrey root is for external use only and is not to be ingested internally or used on deep wounds. Although comfrey does have a long history of internal use and some herbalists still do recommend internal consumption today, research in the past few decades has revealed the presence of toxic constituents that are potentially damaging to the liver. These constituents, known as pyrrolizidine alkaloids (PAs) are present in the roots and leaves of comfrey. Thus, it is prudent to avoid internal use. If one wants to ingest the healing benefits of this plant, I recommend working with comfrey as a homeopathic. This can be purchased at any co-op or supplement store and does not come with any of the health risks.

Note: The following recommendations are for topical use only.

Comfrey knits bones. Another of comfrey's common names is knit bone, referring to the miraculous ability of this plant to "knit" tissue back together after break, fracture, or damage. This applies to broken bones as well as sprains, strains, deep bruises, and any injury to ligament, tendon, or connective tissue. Comfrey stimulates the body's ability to re-knit these tissues back together.

Comfrey weaves skin. Comfrey also "knits" skin tissue back together after damage and is a vulnerary par excellence.

Containing both mucilage and allantoin, a constituent also found in aloe vera, comfrey is incredibly healing and regenerative to skin tissue. **Safety warning**: Comfrey is so stellar in this regard that it should not be applied topically to deep wounds, puncture wounds, or any wounds that have not been thoroughly disinfected first. If you have any doubt about this, simply do not use comfrey.

Comfrey is a weaver. Comfrey's ability to weave and knit damaged tissue back together reflects our own innate capacity to heal and regenerate. Just as it does with physical tissue, comfrey also has this reweaving ability with the spirit. In any kind of healing process, especially one of the deep and challenging variety, let comfrey mirror the miraculous regenerative reweaving ability of Creation, of which you, and comfrey, are a part.

Comfrey is resilient. Anyone who has grown comfrey in their garden knows the incredible resilience and abundance this plant possesses. Comfrey spreads amazingly and will resurface even when you think you've dug up every last root. Not only that, but the leaves that comfrey grows are incredibly nutrient-rich, even serving as an important preparation in biodynamic and other regenerative farming methods. Comfrey grows, sustains, and nurtures the rest of life through her resilience. A worthy capacity to meditate upon.

Comfrey is grandmother medicine. Perhaps it's a function of comfrey's weaving medicine or perhaps it's something else. Either way, the spirit of comfrey always connects me to that ancient lineage of wise grandmothers who knew and know the simple ways of taking care of the people. Perhaps it's because comfrey is simple, easy to grow, ubiquitous, and highly versatile. Comfrey will weave us into the weave that we come from and are woven by: our ancestors and their good simple healing ways.

Infused oil — Dry out the roots before infusing into oil. The mucilage and water content of comfrey roots is too high to be worked with fresh. After drying, whip that oil into a salve to apply to all manner of challenges that need some good old-fashioned knitting medicine.

Flower essence — While not a winter herbal activity, preparing a flower essence from the beautiful scorpioid flowers of comfrey during summer provides a wonderful opportunity to work with the plant. Flower essences work on the subtle, spirit layers of our beings rather than the physical and are prepared in such a manner that eliminates any concern for toxicity. Work with this flower essence whenever you or someone you're serving is in a deep healing process. The healing process might be on the physical, emotional, or spiritual layers. Comfrey works on all of them. Take 3 to 7 drops of the essence 3 to 7x daily to catalyze the deep healing, knitting, and reweaving potential of Creation that this plant holds. You can add the flower essence to your tincture formulas as well to bring in this medicine capacity.

Herbal Formula: Trauma Salve

Note: Not safe for application to deep puncture wounds.

This trauma-healing blend of herbs can be applied to all manner of bodily bumps, such as bruises, breaks, sprains, accidents, injuries, surgeries, and the like. This blend is incredibly anti-inflammatory, healing, and protective to the spirit, which also takes a hit during bumpy times of life.

Prepare an infused oil of equal parts of the following fresh or dried herbs. Then add beeswax to turn into a salve.

Comfrey root
Cottonwood bud
Devil's club inner bark
Self-heal aerial part
St. John's wort flower

Going Deeper into Winter

In the Wild

Nettle root — The rhizomes of stinging nettle have a specifically helpful action on the male prostate.
   * Tincture

Burdock root — These deep taproots cleanse and nourish the liver, kidneys, lymph and digestive systems.
   * Tincture
   * Dry for infusions

Yellow dock root — These rust-colored roots are loaded with iron and make a fabulous blood-cleansing alterative as well as a very reliable laxative.
   * Tincture
   * Dry for infusions
   * Syrup

In the Garden

Echinacea root — Excellent immune stimulant and anti-microbial. My family goes through more echinacea tincture each year than any other herb.
   * Tincture
   * Dry for infusions

Elecampane root — Wildly easy to grow and a helpful decongestant respiratory tonic to have in the apothecary for cold and flu season.
* Tincture
* Dry for infusions

Marshmallow root — This mucilaginous plant is quite easy to grow and yields a big harvest the first year. Excellent digestive healer, throat soother, and cough remedy.
* Tincture
* Glycerite
* Dry for infusions & food

Valerian root — Sleep promoter, pain remedy, and antispasmodic. Easy to grow.
* Tincture
* Dry for infusions

PART 3:
The Magic of Herbal Medicine-Making

"By taking up the competency of handmaking, we are becoming the future ancestors we wished we'd had."

— *Toko-pa Turner, dream teacher and author of*
<u>*Belonging: Remembering Ourselves Home*</u>[1]

Chapter 8:
Making Medicine from the Bodies of Plants

Once we've harvested plants from the Earth, we have three options: We can consume the plants fresh, dry and store them, or process them into medicine. We will cover medicine-making in great detail later on in this chapter. First, let's learn how to properly dry plants as this helps ensure our access to their medicinal properties year-round.

There are many methods for drying out plants, none more preferable than the other. So long as the method accomplishes the goal of properly drying the plant while not decreasing medicinal potency, the method is a good one. We can choose a method that works best with the space we have, taking into consideration the size of our space, the temperature and airflow, the climate we live in, and the tools at our disposal. For example, some people have larger homes with extra bedrooms. These folks might choose to lay their herbs out on a towel on an unused bed. Folks in smaller homes might want to utilize vertical space by hanging plants in bundles from rafters, from shelves high up, or from clotheslines hung across the room.

Plants dry best in cool-ish, dark-ish places with good airflow. No matter the chosen method, the three nemeses that hinder the process of properly drying plants are:

* Inadequate airflow
* Excess moisture
* Exposure to direct sunlight

Methods of Herb Drying

Bundle method — Tie plants into bundles and hang them somewhere in the house out of direct sunlight, taking care not to wrap too many plants per bundle as this could cause the inner plant material to retain moisture and spoil the whole batch.

Sheet method — Spread plants out on a sheet or towel in the house out of direct sunlight, laying them in a single layer to prevent the lower layers from spoilage.

Dehydrator method — These work great to dry plants quickly.

Oven method — Lay herbs in a single layer on a cookie sheet and place them in the oven under the light. The warmth from the light speeds up the drying process and saves space in the home. Just make sure not to forget about the plants and accidentally preheat the oven!

Drying screens — We can make our own drying screens by lining a wood square with chicken wire and laying plants out on the screen.

Build your own drying rack — Even fancier than drying screens, we can make our own drying rack by building a frame to hold multiple layers of removable drying screens.

Mesh drying shelves — Inexpensive and fabulous mesh drying shelves are available that hang from the ceiling. These allow space for a lot of plant material while occupying a minimal footprint.

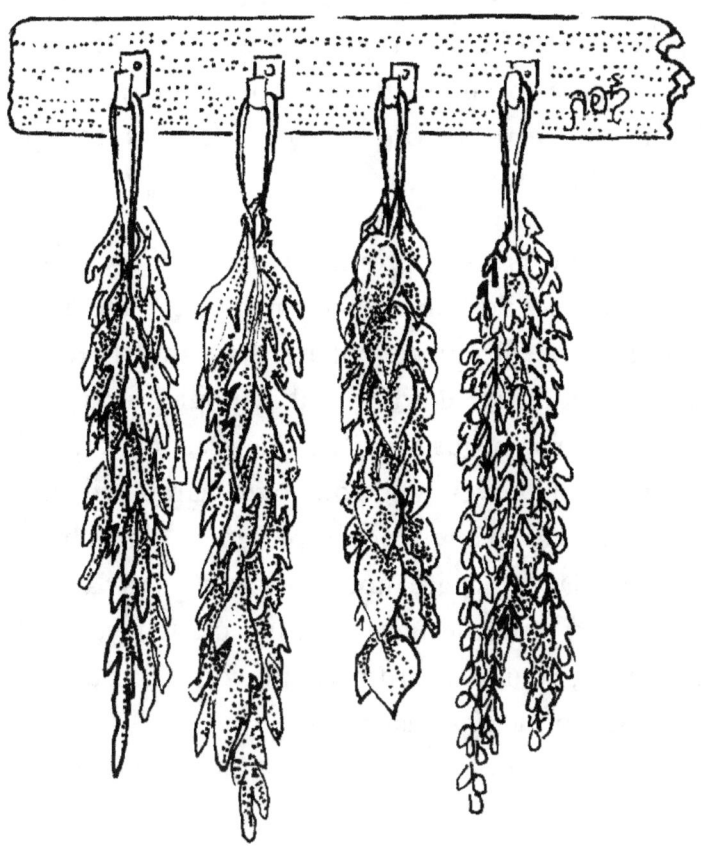

The Bundle Method of drying herbs is a great space saver.

Storing Dried Herbs

Dried plants want to be stored in a well-sealed jar out of direct sunlight and away from a direct heat source. The same nemeses of the drying process hold true during storage. Keep tightly sealed jars away from excess moisture, sunlight, and direct heat. If these guidelines are followed, the general rule of thumb is that dried plants have a shelf life of one year. This makes intuitive sense when we consider the grand plan of nature in which the plants and the people support one another. Each year, at one stop upon the wheel, humans have the opportunity to harvest a plant. Therefore, we need that plant's medicine to last us through one whole turn of the wheel, or one year, before nature offers us the plant's medicine again.

As always, there are exceptions to this. For example, the nettles that were wild harvested over one year ago are likely going to still be far more potent than the dried nettles available for purchase at the local natural grocer, so they shouldn't be thrown out after the one-year mark. Anything that we grow or harvest with our own hands will have an energetic link to us that will not be present in plants harvested by strangers. Plants that are more fibrous, such as barks, seeds, and roots, tend to last longer, even up to a few years. Plants that are daintier, such as aromatic flowers, tend to dwindle sooner, closer to the one-year point.

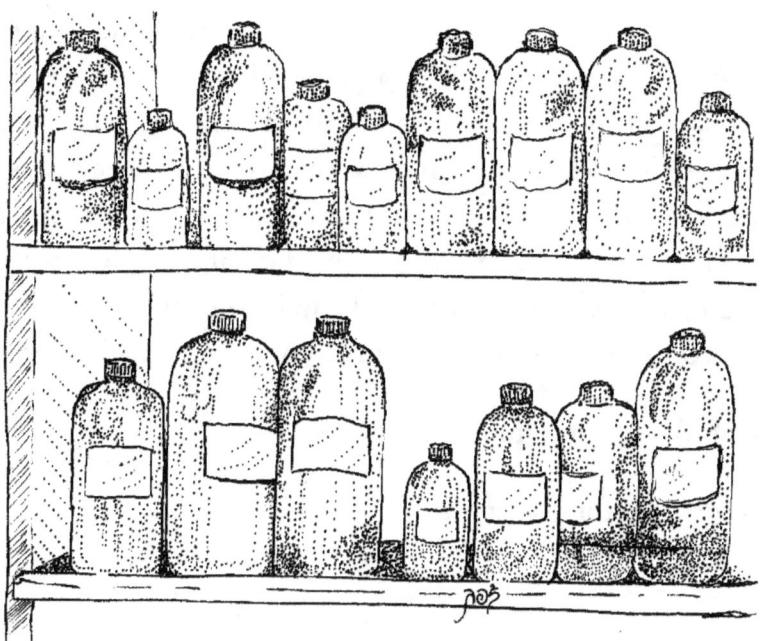

Few things are more satisfying than shelves filled with bottles of herbal medicines created by our own hands and hearts.

The What and Why of Herbal Medicines

Fresh or dried plants are processed into various medicinal preparations primarily for the purpose of preservation. Refrigeration was only invented around a century ago. Until that time, our ancestors needed ways to preserve the healing medicines they harvested from the Earth. Recall that a plant is at peak medicinal potency during one small window of the whole wheel of the year. If we want to have access to that medicine at another time during the year, the plant either needs to be properly dried or preserved by some other method. We prepare tinctures, teas, oils, and the like to preserve the medicine for the rest of the year.

A good medicinal preparation must extract and preserve medicinal constituents from a plant. This is where we enter the realm of menstruums, an old word meaning "the solvent that holds something in suspension." In other words, menstruums are the liquids, solvents, or substances that serve the dual purpose of *extracting* the medicinal constituents from a plant and *preserving* the medicinal potency. Some of the most commonly used menstruums include the following.

Alcohol — for tinctures

Glycerin — for glycerites

Honey — for miels

Oil — for herbal oils

Vinegar — for acetracts

Water — for infusions and decoctions

When plant material is soaking in a menstruum for the purpose of extraction, the term used to describe that process is maceration. During maceration, the menstruum pulls out the medicinal constituents from a plant and suspends them in solution. To understand this concept, consider making a cup of tea. We have to leave the tea bag in the water for enough time for the water to actually pull the constituents into the solution. The water serves as the menstruum that is macerating the herbs in the tea bag.

Medicine-Making Tools

Thankfully, most of the necessary tools for medicine-making already have a place in our kitchens, the following list is all we need.

Stainless steel cooking pot — For heating oils and honeys, making salves, and using a double boiler setup.

Glass measuring cups of various sizes — For measuring menstruums, using a double boiler setup, and easily pouring off finished creations.

Stainless steel mixing bowls of various sizes — These are handy to have around for mixing teas and other dried blends, using as a double boiler setup, and whatever else might be needed in a pinch.

Wooden spoon — For mixing everything!

Fine double mesh strainer — Sometimes lined with cheesecloth, sometimes used alone, strainers strain all our macerations into finished herbal creations.

Potato press/ricer — Available from kitchen stores, these make the straining process infinitely easier and more efficient.

Cheesecloth — For straining off herbal creations into their finished medicinal forms.

Funnels — For pouring creations into their final resting jars without spills.

Kitchen scale — For weighing dried herb quantities, menstruum amounts, and beeswax for salves.

Coffee grinder — For grinding and powdering herbs. A separate grinder for herbs is recommended or else our creations will smell like coffee.

Jars of various sizes — To hold all our macerating and finished herbal preparations, keep a variety of glass jars on hand. Old spaghetti sauce, kraut, jelly, and pickle jars all work well. Thrift stores usually have old mason jars for less than $1 each.

Labels — It's important to label all of our preparations. When first beginning, we might feel confident that we'll remember everything we create, but as time goes on and the herbal collection grows, labels become essential.

Labels include the name and part of the plant, if it was prepared fresh or dry, the menstruum used, and the date it was created.

The Spirit of Medicine-Making

The experience of turning plants into beautiful medicinal preparations is a magical process indeed. Something happens in and to the wild soul when engaged in the process of herbal medicine-making. It conjures up often lost and ancient soul parts who knew and know that *this is what we humans are supposed to do*. There is a deep feeling of rightness in it. When we treat our medicine-making as a soulful endeavor, it becomes sacred space. The steps below can help invoke that divine spirit into the process. We should make certain to add the flair of our own unique dance with spirit and the divine into the creative act.

1. Prepare the space. It's best to work in a clean and decluttered kitchen. This is for hygienic purposes, which are essential to medicine-making success. A clean space also energetically lessens distraction, helping invoke the divine spirit of medicine-making in more of its purity. A clean space helps grant us the freedom to surrender into the process.

2. Gather all supplies. Assemble everything necessary to complete the herbal preparation from start to finish. Gathering our tools ahead of time also increases our ability to surrender and focuses our energy on the magic at hand.

3. Ground and center. It's best to not make medicine when we're "in a state." This does not mean that we must be perfect, pure, and enlightened in order to make medicine. It does mean, however, that if we are especially angry, enraged, sad, annoyed,

frustrated, or distracted by other elements of life, *in a state that we can't shake*, it's a good idea to either choose another time to make medicine or take some extra time before beginning.

4. Pray. If we have a spiritual or religious tradition, we can call on that tradition to hold us in a sacred container as we make our medicine. From the heart, we can send out a prayer that the medicine-making process and the medicine itself be blessed. This act of prayer is powerful, elevating the medicine to the level of spirit and soul. Though we are welcome to pray whatever prayers are aligned with our tradition, a beautiful and simple prayer is, "May this be good medicine for all it touches. May it serve all of life."

5. Connect to the plants. Throughout the whole medicine-making process, we should give ourselves total freedom to vibe in the love, connection, and gratitude we feel toward the plants for offering their bodies in this manner. We can open our hearts to feel the spirits of the plants working with us as we enter into a true co-creative dance, together working to bring healing medicine forward to the people on behalf of all of life.

6. Have fun! Medicine-making is a juicy, sensual, and often ecstatic process. It invokes ancient memories of stirring cauldrons with the forces of life, the plant spirits, and fellow wise ones. Medicine-

making does something to the deep wild soul. Our only job is to get our minds out of the way and let this happen. We can sing if we're called to, play music and dance if we're so moved, laugh from our bellies, sway our hips, and let ourselves be moved by the process. This makes for juicy medicine. Juicy medicine makes for juicy people.

Perhaps as we garble the plants and infuse them into menstruums, we are also garbling our own wild souls. Perhaps while we perform this ancient plant alchemy, we ourselves are also being alchemized into more of who we are at our core. We and the plants are one and the same.

Chapter 9:
Herbal Preparations

Choosing Menstruums

How do we decide which menstruums to utilize in our medicine-making? There are many factors to consider and we all develop our own flair over time. However, as we're first trying our hand at making and taking herbal medicines, it can be helpful to think through a few considerations. Do we want to ingest this herb internally or apply it topically? If we want to ingest the herb, we will choose preparations meant for internal use. These include tinctures, syrups, glycerites, extracts, and dried herbs prepared as infusions or in food. If we want to apply the herb topically, we will consider making infused oils, salves, liniments, or dried herbs prepared as compresses.

Shelf Life

Our next consideration is how long we would like the prepared remedy to last as each preparation has a slightly different shelf life. If we would like the medicine to last many years, then tinctures will be the choice. For topicals, we might choose to turn our oils into salves to increase the shelf life from one to a couple of years. If we're alright with preparations that last only around one year, we will choose glycerites and dried herbs prepared as infusions for internal use and infused oils for external use. The preparations that have an even shorter shelf life of just a few months include syrups, extracts, and miels.

Many years — tinctures, liniments

Couple of years — infused salves

One year — glycerites, dried for infusions, infused oils

A few months — syrups, extracts, miels, acetracts

Another major consideration is a simple and honest assessment of how we prefer to take our medicines. What is already "in our flow" will have the highest compliance. For example, if we love drinking tea, then we will likely move through lots of dried herbs and it would be wise to lean in that direction. Are we kitchen wizards? If so we might end up making more syrups, vinegars, and miels to integrate into our food creations. Are we on-the-go-type people, preferring to just pop our medicine quickly? If so then tinctures might be more in our flow. An honest assessment of what does and does not work for us will help us lean into the life rhythm that has already been established, creating a higher likelihood that the herbs will find their way into the heart of our homes, our lives, and our bodies.

The Basic Folk Formula

As discussed, we will be focusing on what's known as the folk method of medicine-making, a method that is simple and easy to remember. Regardless of the plant or menstruum we are working with, the basic folk medicine-making process is the same. If we can memorize this basic formula, integrating it into our mental repertoire, we will be well set on the path toward becoming competent folk medicine makers.

1. Garble the plants. Process them into their proper and most potent medicinal form, making sure to chop them up into pretty small pieces for maceration as this helps the menstruum penetrate cell walls to extract the medicinal constituents.

2. Fill a pint- or quart-sized glass jar between one-half to two-thirds full of finely chopped plant material. The amount will depend on how much the plant will expand in the menstruum. This is where some experience and a more intimate knowledge of the plants' bodies come in handy. Some plants, and some plant parts, are more likely to swell and increase in size when added to a liquid menstruum, while others do not swell at all. This wisdom comes with trial and error and every plant is different. In general, dried plants expand much more than fresh plants when added to liquid menstruum. Dried leaves and flowers often swell quite a bit, while roots, barks, and seeds tend to not absorb too much menstruum.

3. Pour menstruum over the plant material until it is completely covered with an additional two inches of menstruum above the top of the plant.

4. Label the preparation. Write the plant's name, when it was harvested, where it was harvested, the menstruum used, and the date the maceration process began.

5. Shake, shake, shake! Give the jar a hearty, heartfelt, and joyful shake for a solid handful of seconds. This sacred shake is dual-fold. It helps move the menstruum deeper into the cell walls of the plants to liberate the medicinal constituents and it gives our hearts an opportunity to connect with the heart of the medicine, infusing it with good intentions and good energy.

6. Store the macerating jar in a cool, dry place.

7. Shake or stir the jar every day or as close to every day as possible.

8. After at least two weeks of macerating, strain the contents of the jar through a fine double mesh strainer or potato ricer lined with cheesecloth. A potato ricer can improve the straining process by increasing the yield, sometimes by significant amounts.

9. Store the medicine in a clean, tightly sealed jar or multiple jars. Herbalists often use amber or cobalt jars to store medicinal preparations as these substances reflect and protect from UV light but this is not necessary. If clear glass jars are used, simply make certain to store the jar in a cupboard or other dark place where it is shielded from sunlight.

Herbal Preparations

The Magic of Maceration: Plant material soaks in a menstruum, tightly sealed and shaken every day for an average of two weeks before straining and bottling.

INFUSIONS AND DECOCTIONS

What most people think of as "herbal teas" are called "herbal infusions" by most herbalists. There are actually two types of water-based preparations, herbal infusions and herbal decoctions, with water used as the menstruum in both. Boiling water is used for decoctions. We usually, though not always, utilize hot water to make infusions. The heat helps liberate and extract the medicinal constituents from plants into the water. Heat is catalytic, speeding up the extraction process and making molecules move faster. There are certain mineral-rich plants like nettle and carbohydrate-rich plants like marshmallow that prefer cold-water extractions.

Infusions are made by pouring hot, freshly boiled water over dried herbs, letting them steep for an amount of time, then straining and drinking. We typically use the infusion method when working with the daintier parts of a plant's body, such as the leaves and flowers. These lighter and less fibrous parts of the plant don't need the extra "oomph" of active boiling to make a medicinal-strength cup of tea.

Directions: Steep 1 tablespoon of dried herb in 1 cup of hot water for 15 minutes.

Decoctions are made by actively simmering the dried herbs over heat on the stovetop for an amount of time, then straining and drinking. The decoction method is used when working with sturdier plant parts like barks, roots, and seeds. The denser, more fibrous parts of the plant benefit from the extra heat and energy. The active boiling helps liberate the medicinal constituents.

Directions: Gently simmer 1 tablespoon of dried herb in 1 cup water for 15 minutes.

Dosing Infusions and Decoctions

A good general rule is to steep 1 tablespoon of dried herb per cup of water for 15 minutes. This amount of plant material and amount of time are necessary to bring an herbal infusion or decoction up to a truly medicinal strength. Note that this is a rule of thumb and there are always exceptions depending on a specific plant, person, or situation.

Folks who are brand-new to herbal medicine often under-steep their medicinal herbs. It helps to remember that in order to truly be medicinal strength, the herbs must be steeped for *at least* 15 minutes. This amount of time is required to actually coax the medicine out of the plant and into the water menstruum. Often the suggested steep time is longer, such as 30 to 45 minutes. If the herb is aromatic or has essential oils in it, such as chamomile, peppermint, and lavender, then the infusion needs to be covered while steeping so as to not lose the volatile oils to evaporation.

It is rare that I suggest making only one cup of herbal tea at a time. Instead it is often easier to make the entire day's dosing of tea all at once in the morning, using that basic recipe of 1 tablespoon per cup of water. If attempting to "treat" or really create shifts within our internal ecology, we will likely need to drink 3 to 4 cups of medicinal-strength tea every day. (See page 259 for more info on standard dosing.) By adding 4 tablespoons of herb to 1 quart of water menstruum, steeping for 15 minutes, and then straining, we have made our daily dose of medicine. The jar of tea can be sipped throughout the day. In most instances, it can be drunk either hot or cold.

TINCTURES

Tinctures use alcohol as the menstruum to pull medicinal constituents out of the plant and then preserve the medicine. Finely chopped herbs sit covered in alcohol for at least two weeks, during which the alcohol extracts the medicinal elements. Shaking the jar every day or as often as possible helps to break open the cell walls in the plant, further freeing medicinal constituents. After straining, the medicine has been extracted into the alcohol and is now preserved.

Which Alcohol to Use

Any form of alcohol will work for tincture-making and in some ways, it is up to one's taste and budget. Most herbalists use potato- or grain-based clear spirits like vodka because the neutral flavor provides somewhat of a "blank palette" to carry the herbs. Others prefer brandy due to the complimentary flavor the alcohol imparts to the tincture.

An alcohol menstruum must be at least 25 percent alcohol (50 proof) to be sufficiently preservative. Less than 25 percent alcohol and a tincture could spoil. In the folk method, 80- to 100-proof vodka can be used for all tinctures as this strength extracts most constituents well.

Another option is the use of Everclear, a brand of alcohol that is nearly 200 proof, or close to 100 percent alcohol. This is especially helpful when using herbs whose constituents extract more readily into alcohol, in which case a higher percentage of alcohol will be more desirable. Resins will extract fine in 50 percent alcohol but may extract better in 60 to 75 percent, while carbohydrates may extract better in 30 to

40 percent alcohol. If we want to take the extra step of calculating an exact alcohol percentage to match the constituent profile of a specific plant, the calculations are easy when we consider Everclear to be 100 percent alcohol. For example, if we want to make a 75 percent alcohol tincture to extract the resinous cottonwood buds, then 75 percent of Everclear is mixed with 25 percent water.

A wise woman herbal friend wanted to convince a loved one to take devil's club tincture, feeling strongly that the man would benefit from the plant's adrenal-supportive grandfather energy. However, he was not prone to taking care of himself and the likelihood of compliance was slim to none. But my friend knew the man loved his whiskey. So what did she do? She infused the devil's club into his favorite whisky and just like that, he was sipping his medicine every night, not caring in the slightest that this was a medicinal tincture. Because this wise herbalist honored and flowed with the man's process and way of being, he was now connecting with and ingesting devil's club every day and some healing was underway. The moral of the story is: Do what works!

Liniments

The term "liniment" is used when a tincture is applied topically as opposed to ingested internally. Oftentimes the tincture is soaked in a cloth and then applied to an area for treatment or it is poured directly onto the skin. Liniments are frequently made utilizing witch hazel extract, an alcohol-based menstruum readily available from drugstores, or rubbing alcohol.

Storing Tinctures

Alcohol is an industrial-strength disinfectant par excellence. For this reason, it is highly preservative. Tinctures keep for many, many years without losing potency or spoiling. Store tinctures in a cool dark place out of direct sunlight and away from an active heat source and they will keep for years. Amber or cobalt bottles help protect tinctures from UV light. However, if this is cost-prohibitive or not accessible, tinctures may be stored in any tightly sealed jar out of direct sunlight.

Supplies:
80 to 100 proof vodka, brandy, or liquor of choice
Jar with lid for maceration
Fine double mesh strainer
Cheesecloth
Jars and labels for bottling and storage

Directions: Follow the Basic Folk Method on page 228.

Shelf life: If stored properly, tinctures will last for many years.

GLYCERITES

Glycerine is a wonderful menstruum to substitute for alcohol as some folks, for various good reasons, cannot or prefer not to ingest alcohol-based tinctures. Glycerine is a naturally occurring substance that has a sweet flavor and a syrup-like consistency. The sweet flavor makes it a menstruum of choice for kids' palettes and also brings out the divine taste of certain herbs, such as rose petals and lemon balm. Glycerites generally make herbal extracts much more palatable. Glycerine can be added to alcohol-based tinctures at a ratio of 1 part glycerine to 10 parts alcohol in order to sweeten and smooth out the flavor of particularly strong alcohol plant tinctures.

Glycerine has a much shorter shelf life than tincture extracts made with alcohol, tending to last only 1 to 2 years before beginning to spoil. Storing in the refrigerator does help extend the shelf life.

Where to purchase: Glycerine can be bought in bulk from most herbal apothecaries and health food stores and certainly is available from online distributors of natural products.

Supplies:
Glycerine
Jar with lid for maceration
Fine double mesh strainer
Cheesecloth
Jars and labels for bottling and storage

Directions: Follow the Basic Folk Method on page 228.

Shelf life: Glycerites typically last 1 to 2 years.

ACETRACTS: HERBAL VINEGARS

Acetracts utilize vinegar as the menstruum. Vinegar is especially wonderful at extracting plants that are rich in minerals, such as nettle, dandelion, horsetail, oatstraw, red clover, and alfalfa. Infused vinegars are an easy and delicious way to weave more herbal medicine into food dishes, which is a lovely way of ingesting our medicine. Acetracts are also a great option for folks who don't consume alcohol.

Any vinegar will work as a menstruum. It's really up to taste and budget preferences. For example, folks who like to put balsamic vinegar on their daily salads could benefit from using balsamic for their acetracts to add mineral-rich herbal-infused medicine into their salad dressing. Alternatively, it's often easier to take a "shot" of apple cider vinegar than other vinegars. So for medicinal purposes, apple cider vinegar may be more appropriate. It really depends on our personal taste, preference, the plant, and what we are trying to treat or address.

Supplies:
Vinegar of choice
Jar with lid for maceration
Fine double mesh strainer
Cheesecloth
Jars and labels for bottling and storage

Directions: Follow the Basic Folk Method on page 228.

Shelf life: Acetracts last from six months to a year before starting to turn.

MEDICINAL SYRUPS

A medicinal syrup is made by first decocting plant material and then adding a sweetener, such as honey or sugar. The decoction extracts the medicinal constituents from the herbs. The addition of honey or sugar serves to thicken and preserve the herbs for a longer period of time.

The primary reason to make syrups is simple: They are delicious! This is not always the case for herbal preparations. Syrups are a great way to get herbs into folks with picky taste buds and to convince kids to take herbs. The yummy flavor also means the herbal medicine is easy to mix into foods, smoothies, pour over yogurt or ice cream, etc.

Miels: Herbal Honeys

Miels, or herbal honeys, are another way of utilizing the sweetness and preservative nature of sugar to prepare and preserve our herbal medicines. Herbs are soaked in honey menstruum for at least two weeks, then strained and stored. Similar to syrups, miels are great for sensitive palettes and for weaving into culinary creations.

Supplies:
2 ounces herbs, fresh or dried
1 quart water
Cooking pot
Fine double mesh strainer
Cheesecloth
1 cup honey
Jars and labels for bottling and storage

Directions:

1. Add the 2 ounces of herbs and 1 quart of water to a cooking pot.

2. Simmer the mixture over low heat. A gentle rolling boil is ideal.

3. Simmer in this way until the liquid reduces by one-half, from 1 quart to 1 pint. This usually takes between 40 and 60 minutes.

4. After the liquid has reduced, remove from the heat.

5. Strain the mixture through a strainer lined with cheesecloth.

6. Return the remaining liquid to the pot and return to low heat.

7. Add 1 cup of honey to the liquid.

8. Warm the mixture on low heat until the honey melts. If a thicker syrup is desired, continue to simmer for an additional 20 to 30 minutes.

9. Once cool, bottle the resulting syrup into storage jars.

10. Label and store in the refrigerator.

11. Enjoy within about three months.

Shelf life: If stored in the fridge, syrups will last a few months. After that, keep an eye out for any signs of fermentation. If any carbonation is emitted when the jar is opened, the syrup is probably past its prime.

INFUSED OILS

An herbal-infused oil is prepared by macerating plant material in a "fixed oil." Fixed oils are not the same as "essential oils"—also an herbal preparation, though very different—and many people just beginning their herbalism walk can become confused by this. Examples of fixed oils include olive, sunflower, avocado, grapeseed, coconut, jojoba, castor, and safflower. Any fixed oil works for herbal infusions. It is common to use olive oil because it is neutral, not too slimy or too thin, and holds the healing properties of herbs quite well.

Shelf Life of Infused Oils

Because oil is far less preservative than alcohol, oils tend to last about one year. If stored in the fridge, they will last longer. A lot depends on if fresh or dried plant material is used. Fresh will decrease shelf life. How thoroughly the oil was strained also affects shelf life as any amount of remaining plant particulate in the oil after straining will decrease longevity. Cooler storage temperatures will help infused oils last longer.

Fresh or Dry Plants?

Infused oils last longer if dried plant material is used as we aren't mixing oil with the water from the plants, which is a recipe for spoilage. It is also simpler to work with dried plants. However there are some plants, such as St. John's wort, for whom fresh plants are far superior to dried plants. Generally, fresh plants are more potent and vibrant as they have just recently been plucked from the generative and healing Earth.

There are a few workarounds for this. One step is to leave a freshly harvested plant out to dry for just a day or two before infusing it in oil. This bit of time removes a good portion of the water content. Calendula, for example, tends to infuse well in oil with this extra step and still not spoil too quickly. To remove some of the water content after the oil has been infused, leave it exposed to the air on a bit of heat—in a crockpot on low or a double boiler with the lid off, for example. This will evaporate some of the water content.

There are many ways to make herbal-infused oils. Some require heat and some do not. Some are quicker than others. We should choose the method that works best with our time, space, and supply constraints. For folks new to medicine-making, trying out all the methods of infusing oils will expand our experience and comprehension of the medicine-making process.

Method 1: Solar-Infused

This method is the simplest and some might say the "folkiest" method. It calls upon the healing powers and heat of the Sun to assist in the extraction process. It's very similar to making a tincture. The only difference is that the oil is placed in sunlight while macerating as opposed to darkness for tinctures.

Supplies:
Jar with lid for maceration
Enough olive oil, or other fixed oil, to fill the jar
Fine double mesh strainer
Cheesecloth
Jars and labels for bottling and storage

Directions: Follow the Basic Folk Method on page 228 making certain to leave the macerating jar in a place with plenty of sunlight.

Shelf life: With lots of variability, herbal oils last one year on average.

Method 2: Crock Pot

This method yields an exquisite herbal-infused oil that is medicinally ready in only 1 to 3 days. The application of heat over a long period of time works beautifully for sturdier plant parts like roots and barks, making for a very strong oil.

Supplies:
Glass jar with lid
Enough olive oil, or other fixed oil, to fill the jar
Crock pot
Fine double mesh strainer
Cheesecloth
Jars and labels for bottling and storage

Directions:
1. Chop plant material as finely as possible.

2. Fill the glass jar with the plant material until about ⅓ to ½ full.

3. Pour enough oil into the jar to cover the herbs until they are completely submerged, plus an additional 2 to 3 inches above.

4. Cover with a tight-fitting lid.

5. Place the jar in a crock pot filled with water. Turn the crock pot to its lowest setting.

6. Let the plants "cook" for 1 to 3 days, making certain they don't simmer and that there is always water in the pot as hot water is needed to facilitate extraction and the jar of herbs may break if it is heated without being surrounded by water. Turn the crock pot off before bed or when unable to monitor for water evaporation.

7. When finished, strain herbs through a strainer lined with cheesecloth.

8. Bottle resulting oil (now herb-infused!) into storage jars.

9. Label and store in a dark cool place.

Shelf life: Use within the next year.

Method 3: Double Boiler

The Double Boiler Method utilizes heat to speed up the extraction process. Its primary benefit is that you can create a strong herbal oil in under an hour. Close attention must be paid throughout the whole process to make certain that the oil doesn't become so hot that it boils. For most stovetops, the lowest heat setting works to keep the oil warm but not bubbling. However, some ranges are simply too hot and even the lowest setting is too warm. In this case, eyes should be kept on the oil the entire time, turning the stove on and off as bubbles begin to appear. When an infusing oil gets too hot, it both denatures the composition of the fixed oil and can literally deep-fry our herbs—not good for the integrity of the medicinal constituents nor the smell of the finished oil.

Supplies:
Either a ready-to-use double boiler setup or a cooking pot with a stainless steel or glass bowl that is large enough to rest on the rim of the cooking pot, leaving space for water in the pot underneath it
Enough olive oil, or other fixed oil, to cover the herbs
Fine double mesh strainer
Cheesecloth
Jars and labels for bottling and storage

Directions:
1. Chop the plant material as finely as possible.

2. Place the herbs in the stainless bowl, then pour enough oil into the bowl to cover the herbs until they are completely submerged, plus an additional 1 inch or so.

3. Add enough water to the cooking pot so that the water is a couple of inches below where the bottom of your glass bowl will sit.

4. Create a "double boiler" setup wherein the glass bowl containing the herbs and oil is resting within the cooking pot.

5. Place the double boiler on the stovetop.

6. Heat the herb and oil mixture for 30 to 60 minutes while keeping a close eye on the oil, making certain the oil does not overheat, bubble, or boil. Usually a very gentle rolling boil of the water is ideal for maintaining a good temperature.

7. When finished, strain herbs through a strainer lined with cheesecloth.

8. Bottle the infused oil into storage jars.

9. Label and store in a dark cool place.

Shelf life: Use within the next year.

HERBAL SALVES

Salves, also known as ointments, are made by mixing an herbal-infused oil with beeswax or some other lipid-hardening agent to make it firm. Salves are satisfyingly easy to make. Most people are surprised when they discover how simple the process is.

Salves are a fabulous way to apply herbs topically. Their hardened quality makes them easier to administer than straight oil and they are less likely to cause a mess or stain. The addition of beeswax expands the salve's healing properties due to its antiseptic, vulnerary nature. Salves also last longer, sometimes many years, due to the preservative nature of beeswax. Bricks of beeswax can be grated as needed with a cheese grater or purchased as pastilles, which are very easy to work with.

Supplies:
Cooking pot
Glass measuring cup
Glass jar with lid
1 cup herbal infused oil or unmedicated fixed oil of your choice
1 ounce beeswax, pastilles or grated
Wooden spoon
Fine double mesh strainer
Cheesecloth
Small glass jars or tins and labels

Note: Convenient salve jars include small 4-ounce jelly jars found at most grocery stores or ointment jars found at most apothecaries or natural grocers.

Directions:
1. Prepare an infused herbal oil using one of the three methods shared in the Infused Oils section (see page 242). If an infused oil isn't available, choose one of the other options for medicinal herbal salves listed below.
2. Fill the cooking pot with enough water to reach about halfway to the top of the glass measuring cup.
3. Place the measuring cup inside the pot with water to create a "double boiler" setup.
4. Add herbal oil and beeswax to the glass measuring cup. To each cup of herbal oil, add 1 oz of beeswax.
5. Heat on the lowest setting until the beeswax melts completely, stirring constantly and making sure the mixture doesn't get too hot and cause the oil to bubble.
6. Once the beeswax is fully melted, remove the mixture from heat.
7. Stir in any essential oils, flower essences, or powders now that the mixture is no longer being heated.
8. Pour into small glass jars or tins.
9. Label and store in a cool dark place.

Shelf life: Use over the next couple of years.

Other Ways to Medicate Herbal Salves

There are many ways to weave the healing gifts of the herbs into salves beyond the use of herbal oils. Here are some other ideas.

Add tinctures to salve — Add 5 droppersful of herbal tincture per fluid ounce of herbal oil in a salve. Add the tincture to the mixture as the beeswax is still melting as this allows time for some of the alcohol to evaporate.

Add essential oils to salve — Add 10 to 30 drops of essential oil per fluid ounce of herbal oil in a salve. Add the essential oils after the wax has melted and the mixture has been removed from the heat.

Add flower essences to salve — Add 1 to 10 drops of flower essence per fluid ounce of herbal oil in a salve. Adding the drops after the oil has been removed from heat may help preserve the subtle energies of the essence. Note that only 1 drop is needed to imbue the energy and magic of the essence into the salve.

HERBAL BATHS

Adding herbs to baths is a powerful and often underutilized way of working with herbs. We are literally cooked or steeped in the healing gifts of the plants in an herbal bath. It's a wonderful means of administering herbs for decreasing inflammation, soothing the skin, settling the nerves, promoting circulation, decreasing mucus and congestion, and more. Spiritual bathing with herbs is a practice we see all over the world, recommended whenever we need a cleanse, reset, or reconnection, or when our energy has been thrown off.

Supplies:
Large cooking pot
1 to 2 gallons water
1 cup dried herbs wrapped in a cheesecloth bundle

Directions:
1. Fill a large pot with water and bring it to a boil. The 1 to 2 gallon recommendation is approximate. Essentially, fill a big pot with water.

2. Once boiling, add the 1 cup of dried herbs wrapped in cheesecloth to the hot water.

3. Steep covered for at least 15 minutes, ideally 30 minutes or more.

4. Prepare a bath as usual.

5. After the tea is done steeping, use oven mitts to carry the pot of tea to the bath, pouring it into the bath

water. It's wise to check the temperature and adjust accordingly before putting one's body in the water.

6. Soak in the medicine of the healing plants, letting them wash away, cleanse, and transport us toward healing and wholeness.

Shelf life: Use dried herbs within one year.

FLOWER ESSENCES

In a flower essence, the menstruum is water, with brandy added for preservation. Flower essences differ from the other medicinal preparations shared here in that they do not have medicinal-strength potency. By their nature and intent, flower essences are subtle and work on the subtle layers of our beings. As such, flower essences are not taken for acute physical situations, such as treating a serious infection or relieving acute physical pain. They are taken as spirit medicine, working to shift, unlock, and elevate our own psychospiritual nature into a more radiant and whole state. We work with the flower of a plant whose essence is imprinted into the purest water possible to create a vibrational imprint of the flower into the water. This essence is preserved with 25 percent alcohol, traditionally brandy, and taken in drop doses for spiritual support.

There are many wonderful herbalists whose primary medicine is to create, formulate, and share flower essences. Each time I teach my Intro to Folk Herbalism class, there are usually a few students who meet flower essences and are hooked for life, having found the perfect expression of their own unique herbalism. Once the basic process is understood, we can really run with it. It's very inexpensive to make flower essences as it barely requires any of the plant's bodies and the only cost is the small amount of alcohol used to preserve. It's easy to build a large apothecary of flower essences to share.

Supplies:
Clean, sterilized glass bowl
Enough water to fill the glass bowl halfway
Snips or scissors
Wooden spoon or utensil (optional)
Brandy or other alcohol for preservation
Amber bottles for bottling and storage

Directions:
The Western world was introduced to flower essences by Dr. Edward Bach, a British medical doctor who lived around the turn of the 20th century. Dr. Bach taught that flower essences are to be made on completely sunny days when there is not a cloud in the sky, the idea being that only the energy of the plant, the water, and the Sun should be in the medicine. In my Pacific Northwest rainforest home, cloudless days are hard to come by, so I've bent this rule of Dr. Bach's many times, still yielding beautiful results. So much of flower essence making is intention-driven. When living in cloudy and rainy locations, intend that the space is sacred and pure, and with the grace and blessing of nature it shall be so. The energy of the day, the place, and the essence-maker all feed into the essence's medicine. Flower essences help us to weave the flowering beauty of the plants into our lives, bodies, spirits, and homes in a truly sustainable manner.

1. Fill a glass bowl with water. Use the purest water available and bring this bowl of water to the spot where the essence will be created.

2. Use snips or scissors to cut the flowers directly from the plant's body so that they fall into the bowl of water, allowing them to float on top of the water.

3. If at all possible, it's best if we don't touch the plant's body with our own hands and fingers. Let the scissors do the work. This helps keep our energy out of the essence and the plant's essence in as pure a state of its own nature as possible.

4. Place the bowl with flowers floating on the water in a sacred spot in the Sun if it's a sunny day.

5. Let the bowl sit for a few hours. During this time, the flowers are imprinting their essence into the water. We essence-makers can do whatever our intuition guides us to do during this time. Sometimes we may be guided to leave the essence alone with the wild and come back a few hours later. Some essence-makers will stay near the essence and do prayers, blessings, songs, and invocations during this time. Some will sit in deep communion with the plant and make notes on the conversations about the plant's medicine and messages. Do whatever arises naturally from the wild heart.

6. After the essence is imprinted, it's time to remove the flowers. Use the snips/scissors, a wooden spoon, or some other utensil (ideally one that has been ritually smudged) to remove them. Return them to rest upon the Earth with a blessing.

7. Preserve this essence water with alcohol to create a 25 percent alcohol solution. For example if you have 1 cup of essence water, you will want to add 1/3 cup of brandy to adequately preserve.

8. This essence is now called the "mother essence" and is likely our lifetime supply. Store the mother essence in an amber bottle out of direct sunlight and heat.

9. When ready to dispense a flower essence, take only a few drops of this mother essence and add it to what's known as a "stock bottle." A stock bottle is a small amber bottle with a dropper top. The rest of the stock bottle is filled with a mixture of 75 percent water and 25 percent brandy.

Dosing Flower Essences

Flower essences are taken in drop doses at 3 to 7 drops 3 to 7x daily or however frequently we are guided by our inner wisdom. With drop dosing, we ingest single drops as opposed to whole dropperfuls (one dropperful is equal to roughly 30 drops), so the amount of liquid is much smaller. They can be taken on or under the tongue, diluted in a sip or glass of water, added to sprays or baths, or anointed onto the body. The possibilities are endless.

Shelf life: If stored properly, tinctures will last for many years.

Chapter 10:
Plants as Medicine

Do Herbs Work?

As the years of herbal crafting go by, our shelves continue to fill with tinctures, oils, dried herbs, smudge bundles, and salve jars. It's not uncommon to continually outgrow our "herbal area," starting with one shelf in one cupboard, to taking over the kitchen, to perhaps one day having our very own home apothecary room. When we are first starting out, a question always arises: "I have all of these beautiful medicinal jars lining my shelves, but how exactly do I use them?" Good question. As my late mentor Tierney Salter used to say, "Herbs work . . . if you take them!" This chapter is all about dosing herbs.

Safety first: If someone is pregnant or breastfeeding, has pre-existing medical conditions, or is on any pharmaceutical medications, they should always consult with a medical provider before ingesting anything.

There are as many schools of thought around dosing herbs as there are herbalists practicing herbalism. On one end of the spectrum are herbalists who only work with drop dosing and on the other are herbalists who only work with full-strength manufactured herbal products standardized to specific percentages of active ingredients. Below is a useful starting point from which to work as we are deepening our knowledge, wisdom, and embodied experience with herbs. In truth, dosing always varies with each person, their state of health, and the plants being ingested, as well as many other factors.

Simpling

Referred to as "simpling" by many herbalists, taking herbs as a single, or one at a time as opposed to in a formula, is a wonderful way of working with the healing gifts of herbs. If a plant is really the perfect fit for a person in a particular situation, then ingesting it by itself can create a powerful healing link. I often work with simpling when working on the more energetic or spiritual layer of health, inviting the plant in as a teacher-ally-healer to align me or someone I'm helping toward a specific healing or learning shift.

What Is a Dropperful?

The recommended dosing for most herbs is listed in "droppersful." One dropperful is considered to be *the amount of liquid that enters the pipette when you squeeze the top once.* This usually equates to about 30 drops, with one drop being equal to one milliliter.

Drop Dosing

"Drop dosing" refers to the act of ingesting tinctures one drop at a time as opposed to working in whole droppersful. Dosing recommendations may be listed as drops, such as "10 drops taken 3x daily." In these instances, it is essential to count the drops out one-by-one for each dosing. This way of taking herbs is often indicated when we are working at the spirit or energetic layers as full-strength dosing is not necessary to create the necessary shifts.

Dosing recommendations are broken up into three categories: chronic physical health issues, acute physical health issues, and spiritual support. Note that these three categories overlap and interweave and each case should be considered individually.

Chronic Health Issues

Chronic health issues are those that last for three months or longer, are persistent, long-lasting, and may get worse over time. They tend to bring limitations to our daily quality of life. Because they have taken a longer time to build, they often take a longer time to heal as they require a slow and steady shifting of the inner ecology to return the system to a more balanced state.

Examples of chronic health issues include adrenal fatigue, stress and mood imbalance, hormonal imbalance, liver or kidney challenges, chronic skin issues, chronic inflammation, and cardiovascular health.

For chronic health issues, consider taking average doses of herbs over longer periods of time.

Tincture — 2 droppersful 3x daily or 3 droppersful 2x daily

Tea — 3 to 4 cups daily at a strength of 1 tablespoon steeped per cup of water

Acute Health Issues

Acute health issues are severe and sudden in their onset. They come on fast, need to be addressed fast, and are limited in their duration.

Examples of acute health issues include the onset of cold or flu, severe pain, sinus infection, headache, acute anxiety, panic, or insomnia, urinary tract or yeast infection, and toothache.

In acute situations, consider taking lower doses of the herbs more frequently. The more regular dosing keeps the body saturated with the healing properties of the herbs in order to hopefully wave off the worsening symptoms of a rapidly unfolding acute issue.

Tincture — 1 to 2 droppersful 4 to 6x daily

Tea — ¼ cup served up to 8x daily

Spiritual Support

When working at the spiritual layer of health, the dosing is much lower. Taking drop doses or even simply holding or wearing a plant can facilitate powerful spiritual healing shifts. This in turn can affect our physical health as spiritual, emotional, and physical health are all interrelated.

Examples of spirit support include heart opening and clearing, energetic protection, personal empowerment, soul-level healing, and integration.

Tincture or flower essence — 3 to 7 drops 3 to 7x daily

Tea — Amount may be very light, with just a pinch of the herbs, taken intentionally throughout the day.

Fresh or dried herb — Wear or carry a pinch of the plant's body in a medicine bag or place it on an altar and meditate or pray with it.

Oil or flower essence — Anoint different parts of the body, such as the heart, third eye, or belly, with an oil or essence of the plant.

Formulating

Formulating, or blending herbs into synergistic blends, is an art and skill that herbalists develop over time. Formulating requires an intimate knowledge of the flavors, medicinal properties, and overall personality of each of the plants. Like any good sturdy relationship, these bonds and deeper understandings of one another take time to unfold and grow strong roots. As our relationship and experience with the plants deepen, over time we all develop our own "flair" for formulating that is unique to us and our unique walk with the plants.

The way we begin to build these relationships is by practicing. Just give it a go! Try mixing herbs together into a tea blend and see how they taste and make us feel. Sure, we will make formulas that taste awful, don't go down well, and just don't feel quite right. But so long as we have basic safety considerations in mind, the worst that can happen is that we make a yucky-tasting tea—and this is how we learn.

Here are some questions to ponder as we begin to put our own formulas together.

What is the chief complaint or the healing intention? What would you like the formula to achieve? Give the formula a name, such as Mood Balancer, Heart Healer, Sinus Support, etc. This naming helps hone and clarify the formula's intention and is a very real part of the medicine that we ingest.

Which body systems need to be addressed? Having some basic knowledge of anatomy and physiology on the herbal path is quite helpful. The body systems include the skeletal, muscular, nervous, endocrine, cardiovascular, lymphatic, respiratory, digestive, urinary, and reproductive systems. Identifying which systems the formula should support, cleanse, invigorate, and tonify helps to create a well-balanced and powerfully acting formula.

What medicinal actions are needed? See the glossary on page 273 for full descriptions of medicinal actions. Identify which medicinal actions are needed to support the healing intention and the body systems involved.

How much do mental, emotional, and spiritual issues play into the picture? After flushing out the medicinal actions and body systems with beneficial herbs, consider adding a bit of a plant whose spirit medicine can help balance and facilitate the larger soul process at play.

In what form would the herbs be most potent and best treat the situation? Some menstruums extract certain constituents from plants more optimally, so make sure to think this through. For example, we may really want to ingest nettle. Doing so in tea form is going to be much stronger than in tincture form.

Which herbal preparation will have the best compliance? Kids typically don't like ingesting things that taste bad and that sometimes includes kids of all ages. Be nonjudgmental and honest about what we, or whomever the formula is for, will and will not ingest with regularity, then choose preparations accordingly. Sensitive palettes typically like glycerites, syrups, and sweetened teas. Some people can't ingest alcohol. Some people don't like drinking teas, while others love them. Flow with the preference, the palette, and the life of whomever the medicine is for.

Can all the healing goals be met or should we consider breaking it up into more than one formula? This is a common conundrum as there are often many herbs we want to include in a formula to cover all the medicinal actions and body systems. Sometimes it's best to break it up into two formulas. Oftentimes one formula for general nerve and adrenal support is indicated, with a second separate formula that is more targeted to treat the specific condition. Sometimes we can break it up into one tea and one tincture.

Recipe Box

From our very first formulation explorations, it's wise to grow the habit of writing down each and every recipe we create. A recipe book or box that holds note cards both work beautifully to house these precious herbal notes. Documenting all of our formulas in this way helps us track our expanding learning process, provides a place for notes on what did and did not work, and allows us to repeat those recipes that produced great results. We can then pass this tome, a sacred and treasured resource, down to future generations of herbalists in our families so they can pick up right where we left off.

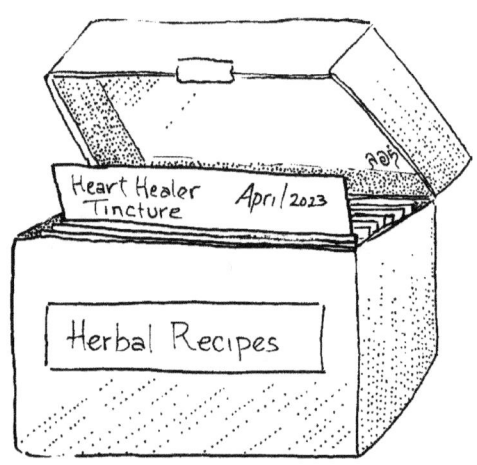

The herbal recipe box grows into a precious jewel of healing wisdom to refer to and pass along to those who follow our footsteps.

Conclusion: Toward a Re-Membered World

The Council Table

There are countless traditions of herbalism, each with its own cosmology and terminology. In the original design of things, herbalism sprouted directly from the Earth, where the people and the plants co-resided. Thus we find that there are as many methods of herbalism as there are cultures on this Earth. This diversity is a beautiful thing. The Earth loves our diversity. Even among "modern" practices of herbalism, the diversity is vast. Today in wide practice there is Ayurveda, Traditional Chinese Medicine, Unani-Tibb, vitalism, physiomedicalism, and folk, just to name a few. What we know as the "Western Tradition" today is really a very recent mash-up of many of these slightly older traditions that are nonetheless still born of the modern mind.

Though the diversity is beautiful, it can sometimes be overwhelming for the beginner's mind when they first embark on their journey. Innocent herbal-seekers set out with a pure heart—a longing in their bones to connect with the Earth and practice medicine with her plants—only to become utterly lost by the overwhelm of choosing a tradition to follow. What do we do with this overwhelm?

Here is a regular spiritual practice I have that may be helpful, called the Council Table. It is similar in spirit to the Native American medicine wheel and is also inspired by the Round Table of King Arthur, Camelot, and the ancient Celtic world.

The Council Table is huge and round and we can imagine ourselves seated there as members of the council. The circular nature of the table teaches that all voices at the Council Table are equal, with none above the other. Each seat at the table is valid, right, and true. It simply has a different perspective or voice to bring to the conversation. Each voice is necessary for the good of the whole.

Let's imagine that this quandary of so many herbal traditions and paths is brought to council. The table is surrounded by herbalists from all over the world from many different walks of life. Each practices a very different style of "herbalism" based on the land they reside in, the culture that informs them, and the lineages that run through their blood.

The Council Table reminds us to value all voices, perspectives, lineages, and traditions and to understand that none is more right than the other. It reminds us that herbalism is "allying with the plants to bring healing to the people" and that this spirit can be made manifest in countless ways. Though the words, plants, and practices may differ, the spirit at the center of each tradition is the very same. The job of an herbalist is simply to find where the truth lies in their own heart and mind. Each herbalist at the table has followed their own threads of lineage, location, and life circumstance. Amidst this vast diversity, each member at the Council Table respects and honors all others, recognizing that each is necessary for the good of all.

This Council Table concept can be helpful as we encounter the many differing viewpoints and belief systems at the beginning of the journey of herbalism. Instead of going into overwhelm, let us imagine ourselves at this Council Table. Our individual walks are born out of our life experience, our teachers, our longings and feelings of rightness, our conversations with the Earth and the plants, and our sacred intentions for walking this path. We can bless all others on their own unique walks and be grateful for their voices at the Council Table, for it is only with everyone's piece that the puzzle of Creation can be complete.

Perhaps this Council Table meditation can be useful for other quandaries as well, reaching far beyond the small question of diversity in herbalism. Perhaps this table where all beings have a seat might help lead the Earth and her humans forward into a re-membered world. I believe the council, or rather the spirit that underlies and informs it, is an essential piece of the medicine bridge that will lead to the new world we are all birthing together. Herbalism too will walk along that medicine bridge into the new Earth.

Life Feeds Life

A great blessing on the herbal path is that the sense of soul excitement and wonder never leaves us. Instead, life often expands into ever more enchantment. There is an infinite well of wisdom and knowledge to drink from, a forever unfurling spiral of more connection, wisdom, healing, and homecoming. Boredom is not a companion on the herbal journey and the blessings are many, making for a rich and deeply connected life in which new plant friends find us wherever we travel.

And there is always more to learn. As herbalists, each year we gather more insight into the plants, their subtleties, their quirks, where they like to grow, with whom, in what conditions, what causes them to flower, what critters they like, and on and on. Our intimacy continues to deepen as our embodiment of their mysteries grounds into our very bodies and souls. Remember, this book is meant as a *starter set*, intended to awaken our relationship with the plants and with the seasons and to teach us *how* to orient ourselves to the lifelong path of herbalism. It is the plants who are the true teachers and healers.

Relating to the plants within the seasons nourishes our sense of rootedness, of belonging-ness, a connection to something larger than ourselves. To put it another way, the walk of seasonal herbalism helps us feel simply at home within our lives and in this world in which we live. This sense of rightness and homecoming blossoms when there's an embodied sense of membership within the web of life, a feeling that we do indeed belong, a resonance of truth that all of life is our kin.

As we spiral toward closing, let us take a few moments to breathe into any sense of rootedness and belonging that may have sprouted from our encounter with the seasons and the healing herbs of the Earth. Even if it is the faintest whisper, let us invite that whispering seedling of belonging into the front of our awareness.

Invite and then allow any gratitude we feel to blossom in the space of the heart—gratitude for the plants, the Mother Earth and her seasons, the ancestors, and any other loved ones from the web of life. Let us allow the gratitude to unfurl in our hearts, knowing that *life feeds life* and the life that is this gratitude will continue to grow more life, within our hearts and within this world.

Beam the gratitude and the good dream of a future where all of life is thriving, the waters are clear, the trees are allowed to grow old, the gardens are lush, medicinal plants abound, and the insects and animals are many. Humans are also present in this dream, thriving because they remember their sacred duty: to love and protect all of their loved ones, human and nonhuman kin, on this good green beautiful Earth. The people are kept well and nourished by the blessings of their family members, the healing plants, and all of Creation.

May it be so, in service to all.

Glossary

The following list of terms comprise the common vernacular used among Western herbalists to describe a plant's physical medicine. As herbalists, we seek to deepen our understanding of the question "How does a plant's body affect a person's body?" Learning and integrating the meaning of the following terms helps strengthen our ability to answer that question.

Beneath each term is a list of commonly known and widely used plants that are easy to find and readily available. Those included in this book are marked with an asterisk*.

Adaptogen — Increases the body's ability to cope with stress.
- devil's club*, ginseng, eleuthero, schisandra, tulsi, ashwagandha, spikenard, polypore medicinal mushrooms like turkey tail, artist's conk, and reishi

Alterative — Blood cleansers that improve the body's ability to detoxify by supporting the body's organs and pathways of elimination.
- dandelion*, cleavers*, nettle*, Oregon grape*, burdock, red clover, yellow dock, echinacea, sarsaparilla, gentian, artichoke

Analgesic — Pain relievers.
- cottonwood* (topically), yarrow* (topically), Sitka valerian, California poppy, bleeding heart, pedicularis, willow, kava kava, valerian, Jamaican dogwood, cannabis

Antibiotic — Fights bacterial infection.
- Oregon grape*, yarrow*, red cedar*, cottonwood*, usnea, goldenseal, echinacea, garlic, myrrh, oregano, thyme

Anticatarrhal — Decreases production of mucus.
- yarrow*, nettle*, cottonwood*, red cedar*, Oregon grape*, elder* flower, mullein leaf, usnea, pine needles, eyebright, goldenseal, yerba mansa, yerba santa, colt's foot, sage, thyme

Antifungal — Fights fungal infection.
- red cedar*, calendula*, Oregon grape*, usnea, goldenseal, pau d'arco, calendula, thyme, tea tree, black walnut

Antispasmodic — Relaxes muscle spasms.
- yarrow*, cottonwood*, Sitka valerian, pedicularis, skunk cabbage, black cohosh, black haw, chamomile, cramp bark, kava kava, lobelia

Antiviral — Fights viral infections.
- elder*, Oregon grape*, St. john's wort*, olive leaf, goldenseal, oregano, licorice, lemon balm, astragalus, osha, lomatium, polypore mushrooms like turkey tail, artist's conk, and reishi

Astringent — Constricts, tightens, and tones tissues.
- yarrow*, raspberry*, rose*, nettle*, chickweed*, cottonwood*, Oregon grape*, red cedar*, hawthorn* leaf and flower, blackberry leaf and root, geranium, oak, alder, uva ursi, willow, plantain, bayberry, cinnamon, goldenseal, green tea, sage

Bitter — Stimulates bitter response in taste buds, leading to gastric secretions.
- dandelion*, yarrow*, Oregon grape*, nettle*, burdock, pine needles, artichoke, gentian, hops, horehound, wormwood, motherwort

Bronchodilator — Relaxes bronchial muscles to permit easier breathing.
- hawthorn*, red cedar*, yarrow*, skunk cabbage, pine needles, anise, elecampane, lobelia, ma huang, thyme, yerba santa

Carminative — Reduces gas and bloating.
- yarrow*, juniper, fennel, anise, ginger, cinnamon, peppermint, chamomile, angelica

Demulcent — Soothes and heals internal mucous membranes.
- comfrey*, chickweed*, plantain, marshmallow, slippery elm, flax, corn silk, oatseed, licorice

Diaphoretic — Induces perspiration, breaks fever.
- yarrow*, elder* flower, catnip, boneset, peppermint, hyssop, ginger, thyme, lemon balm

Diuretic — Stimulates urination, cleanses kidneys and bladder.
- cleavers*, dandelion*, nettle*, burdock, uva ursi, corn silk, parsley leaf, celery seed

Emmenagogue — Stimulates menstruation.
- yarrow*, red cedar*, mugwort*, blue cohosh, black cohosh, pennyroyal

Hypotensive — Lowers blood pressure.
- hawthorn*, yarrow*, Sitka valerian, motherwort, green tea, linden, olive leaf, lemon balm, skullcap, cramp bark, cayenne

Laxative — Stimulates bowel movement.
- dandelion root*, burdock, yellow dock, cascara, aloe, marshmallow, rhubarb, senna, psyllium

Lymphagogue — Supports function of the lymphatic system and stimulates lymphatic detoxification and circulation.
- cleavers*, chickweed*, nettle*, burdock, red root, mullein, red clover, echinacea, poke root, ocotillo, wild indigo

Nervine — Supports and nourishes the nervous system.
- St. John's wort*, hawthorn*, yarrow*, California poppy, Sitka valerian, oatseed, catnip, chamomile, lavender, kava kava, skullcap, lemon balm, passionflower, linden, motherwort

Styptic — Arrests bleeding.
- yarrow*, Oregon grape*, raspberry leaf*, oak leaf, alder leaf, shepherd's purse, blackberry leaf, bayberry, cinnamon, goldenseal, witch hazel

Vulnerary — Promotes healing of external wounds.
- comfrey*, chickweed*, St. John's wort*, rose*, cottonwood*, calendula*, plantain, arnica, aloe

End Notes

PART 1
[1] Gladstar, Rosemary. *Rosemary Gladstar's Herbal Recipes for Vibrant Health: 175 Teas, Tonics, Oils, Salves, Tinctures, and Other Natural Remedies for the Entire Family*. North Adams, MA: Storey Publishing, 2008.

Chapter 1
[1] Moss, Robert. *Active Dreaming: Journeying beyond Self-Limitation to a Life of Wild Freedom*. Novato, CA: New World Library, 2011.
[2] Neihardt, John G. *Black Elk Speaks*. Lincoln, NE: University of Nebraska Press, 2014.
[3] Estés, Clarissa Pinkola. *Beginner's Guide to Dream Interpretation*. Audio recording. Louisville, CO: Sounds True, 2003.
[4] Holecek, Andrew. *Dream Yoga: Illuminating Your Life through Lucid Dreaming and the Tibetan Yogas of Sleep*. Boulder, CO: Sounds True, 2016.
[5] Estés, Clarissa Pinkola. "Letter to a Young Activist during Troubled Times: Do Not Lose Heart, We Were Made for These Times." 2008.
[6] Bayo Akomolafe and Marta Benavides. "The Times Are Urgent: Let's Slow Down." Accessed February 7, 2023. https://www.bayoakomolafe.net/post/the-times-are-urgent-lets-slow-down
[7] Berry, Thomas. *Dream of the Earth*. San Francisco, CA: Sierra Club Books, 1988.
[8] Lovelock, James. *Gaia: A New Look at Life on Earth*. Oxford, EN: Oxford University Press, 2016.

Chapter 2
[1] Brooks, Svevo. *The Art of Good Living: Simple Steps to Regaining Health and the Joy of Life*. Boston, MA: Houghton Mifflin, 1990.
[2] Weed, Susun S. *Wise Woman Herbal: Healing Wise*. Woodstock, NY: Ash Tree Publishing, 2003.
[3] United Plant Savers. "United Plant Savers." Accessed February 11, 2023. https://unitedplantsavers.org

Chapter 3
[1] Pojar, Jim and Andy MacKinnon. *Plants of the Pacific Northwest Coast: Washington, Oregon, British Columbia and Alaska.* Vancouver, BC: Lone Pine International, 2016.
[2] Kloos, Scott. *Pacific Northwest Medicinal Plants: Identify, Harvest, and Use 120 Wild Herbs for Health and Wellness.* Portland, OR: Timber Press, 2017.

PART 2
[1] Good Feather, Doug. *Think Indigenous: Native American Spirituality for a Modern World.* Carlsbad, CA: Hay House, Inc., 2021.

Chapter 4
[1] Kloos, *Medicinal Plants.*
[2] Weed, *Wise Woman.*
[3] Holmes, Peter. *The Energetics of Western Herbs: A Materia Medica Integrating Western and Chinese Herbal Therapeutics.* London, EN: Aeon Books, 2020.

Chapter 5
[1] Prechtel, Martín. *Stealing Benefacio's Roses.* Berkeley, CA: North Atlantic Books, 2006.
[2] Moore, Michael. *Medicinal Plants of the Pacific West.* Santa Fe, NM: Red Crane Books, 2003.
[3] Frances, Deborah. *Practical Wisdom in Natural Healing: Sage Advice for Modern Times.* Chandler, AZ: Polycrest Publishing, 2014.

Chapter 6
[1] Frances, *Practical Wisdom.*
[2] Yance, Donald. "Targeting CoV -2019 Utilizing Unitive Medicine – Botanical, Nutritional, Dietary and Lifestyle." 2021.

Chapter 7
[1] United Plant Savers. "Species At-Risk List." July 2022.
[2] Pojar and MacKinnon, *Plants of the Pacific Northwest.*

PART 3
[1] Toko-pa Turner. *Belonging: Remembering Ourselves Home*. Salt Spring Island, BC: Her Own Room Press, 2017.

Appendix

I: Home Herbal Aid Kit

The following list includes herbs, homeopathics, and essential oils that are very useful in family home care. The herbs listed focus heavily on the plants shared in this book, plus a handful of others that are handy, versatile, and easy to find at a local or online apothecary.

Herbs
Arnica — oil
Calendula — tincture, oil/salve, dried
Chickweed — oil/salve
Comfrey — oil/salve
Cottonwood — tincture, oil/salve
Dandelion — tincture, dried root and leaf
Devil's club — tincture, oil/salve
Echinacea — tincture
Elderberry — dried for syrup
Fennel — tincture/glycerite, whole seeds
Garlic — oil
Hawthorn — tincture, dried
Mullein — oil
Nettle — dried
Oregon grape — tincture, oil/salve
Raspberry — dried leaf
Red cedar — tincture, oil/salve, essential oil
Rose — tincture/elixir
St. John's wort — tincture, oil/salve
Yarrow — tincture, oil/salve, dried

30C Homeopathics
Arnica montana
Belladonna
Chamomilla
Pulsatilla

Essential Oils

Relaxing essential oils — Add to baths, diffusers, and body oils for stress and mood, relaxation, sleep support, and general vibes in the home.
- lavender, vetiver, chamomile, ylang ylang, sandalwood, rose, rose geranium

Decongestant essential oils — Add to baths, diffusers, and vaporubs for respiratory challenges, coughs, and sore throats.
- yarrow, rosemary, eucalyptus, thyme, peppermint

II: Resource List

While there are hundreds of fabulous herbals available, there is a great power in keeping things simple. The majority of one's home and community folk herbalism can be accomplished with a just a handful of tried and true resource books – these are my favorites, the ones I return to time and time again.

Herbals
* *Rosemary Gladstar's Herbal Recipes for Vibrant Health* by Rosemary Gladstar
* *Medical Herbalism* by David Hoffmann
* *Herbal Healing for Women* by Rosemary Gladstar
* *Encyclopedia of Natural Healing for Children and Infants* by Mary Bove
* *The Natural Pregnancy Book* by Aviva Jill Romm
* *Practical Wisdom in Natural Healing* by Dr. Deborah Frances

Plant Spirit Medicine
* *Plant Spirit Medicine* by Eliot Cowan
* *Plant Spirit Healing* by Pam Montgomery
* *Plant Intelligence and the Imaginal Realm* by Stephen Harrod Buhner

Medicine-Making
* *Making Plant Medicine* by Richo Cech
* *The Herbal Medicine-Makers' Handbook* by James Green

Pacific Northwest Field Guides
* *Pacific Northwest Medicinal Plants* by Scott Kloos
* *Plants of the Pacific Northwest Coast* by Jim Pojar and Andy MacKinnon

Dreaming
* *Beginner's Guide to Dream Interpretation* audio by Clarissa Pinkola Estés
* *Conscious Dreaming* by Robert Moss
* *The Wisdom of Your Dreams* by Jeremy Taylor
* *Belonging* by Toko-pa Turner
* *The Kin of Ata Are Waiting for You* by Dorothy Bryan

Index

acetracts, 239
arnica, 141
asking permission, 56
balm of gilead, 204
bleeding heart, 140
burdock, 91, 147, 197, 198
calendula, 131
california poppy, 139
cedar, 138, 155, 182
chamomile, 97, 133
chickweed, 83, 198
cleavers, 82, 88, 198
cold and flu care tea, 129
comfrey, 205
dandelion, 91, 198
decoctions, 232
devil's club, 149
dosing, acute, 259
dosing, chronic, 259
dosing, spiritual, 260
dreaming, 37
dreamweaver tea, 97
drop dosing, 258
drying methods, 216
echinacea, 210
elderberry, 170
elderberry syrup, 175
elderflower, 129, 139
elecampane, 275
empowered tincture, 155
fennel, 52, 147, 275
fight the fungus salve, 188
fir, 102
flower essences, 253
flowering nature tea, 133

folk formula, 60, 228
formulating, 261
garbling, 62
ginger, 101, 193
glycerites, 238
grouchies tincture, 123
hawthorn, 58, 161
healthy skin drops, 198
heart hug tincture, 166
herbal baths, 251
horehound, 275
horsetail, 82, 102
huckleberry, 156
infused oils, 242
infusions, 232
juniper, 160
lady's mantle, 103
lavender, 97, 133
lemon balm, 82, 97, 133
liniments, 236
lomatium, 193, 274
love your lymph tincture, 91
marshmallow, 232, 275, 276
medicine-making tools, 221
menstruums, 227
miels, 240
monographs, 64
mugwort, 38, 92, 101
nettle, 77, 101, 210
oatseed, 97
offerings, 36
Oregon grape, 160, 188, 189
peppermint, 82

pine, 274, 275
plantain, 102
quick rose hip jam, 169
raspberry, 98
red clover, 82, 91, 101, 133
rose, 101, 112, 123, 133, 138, 166
roses hips, 167
safety, 60
sage, 103, 138
salves, 248
self-heal, 135, 136, 137
skin-healer salve, 87
skullcap, 52, 276
smudging, 187
spirit reset bath, 138
spring cleanse tea, 82
St. John's wort, 87, 118, 155, 209
syrups, 240
the big guns, 193
tinctures, 235
trauma salve, 209
urinary soother drops, 160
usnea, 193, 274
uva ursi, 160
wheel of the year, 45
wild carrot, 147
wild harvesting kit, 61
wild rose elixir, 117
womb love tea, 101
yarrow, 124
yerba santa, 193

Author's Note

This book came from the world of dreams. Having dreamt three times I had written a book under its title, the message was finally received and I set to weaving it from the Otherworld into this one.

Not entirely sure where the dreams would lead, throughout its birthing process I came to see that this book's unique contribution is to show the great depth available in what might first appear to be "simple." For at its ancient core, herbalism is simply about relationships, and relationships are born in the heart. If we allow the plants to open our hearts, as they inevitably do, we are then given the truly priceless gift of restoring our connection within the very web of life. The reweaving power of love is the strongest medicine we have in this world.

I believe this Great Reweaving to be the task of those of us alive today and have dedicated my life to the cause through my teaching and healing work. I live with my family on the wild lands of Washington state's Olympic Peninsula, where I grow and make medicine and teach classes on dreaming, women's healing, Earth reconnection, and, of course, simple folk herbalism. More info about my work can be found on my website, www.laurelcrownhealing.com.

Seasonal Herbalism is my first book and I pray that it is useful to you, your people, and beyond to all of Creation. May your journey with the plants increase your delight, health, and trust in life. May you protect them as they protect you.

With great blessings,
Lauren Morgan

Artist's Note

I am a lifelong artist, working in a variety of 2D mediums, including all forms of painting, drawing, and printmaking. I earned a degree in visual arts from Eastern Connecticut State University in 1989 while raising my three children. My work has illustrated field guides and a self-published coloring book, and has been selected for the covers of magazines.

Since 2012 I have been exploring a technique of painting known as "mischtechnik," which means "mixed technique" in German and is the style I used to create the cover of this book. Developed by Ernst Fuchs, one of the Fantastic Realist painters of the mid-20th century in Europe, mischtechnik is used in both oil and acrylic painting to create works that are mesmerizing and fantastical.

Art is a way of life for me and the act of creating is my spiritual practice. I take inspiration from the world around me, especially nature. In particular, while illustrating the herbs represented in this book, I had the opportunity to dive deeper into the medicine and magic each one of them brings to us on the beautiful Olympic Peninsula. I am grateful to have been a part of this very special offering.

To view more of my work, visit my website, www.laurenblairchurchill.com.

Artfully yours,
Lauren Blair Churchill